Israel's Administrative Culture

Israel's Administrative Culture

By

GERALD E. CAIDEN

Graduate School of Public Affairs
University of California, Berkeley

1970

INSTITUTE OF GOVERNMENTAL STUDIES

UNIVERSITY OF CALIFORNIA, BERKELEY

$2.75

International Standard Book Number (ISBN): 0-87772-071-1
Library of Congress Catalog Card Number: 70-631727

*Let us be frank. This is a trade we knew
not formerly or, at least, have not followed
for centuries past. We have to practise a
new craft, and almost create something out
of nothing. The spiritual possessions, the
practical experience, and the intellectual
assets we brought from our work in the
Yishuv, in an alien Government and in our
own institutions--these are inadequate. We
must outdo ourselves in a pioneer endeavor,
galvanize the capacity buried deep in our
soul, and deploy to the utmost our traits
of the spirit, ethical and intellectual.
What we did before the State arose is not,
cannot be, enough. We are a small and poor
people, our needs are many and burdensome.
We must fulfill enormous tasks with scanty
means.*

David Ben-Gurion
5712   1952

Contents

Foreword

Regardless of sharply conflicting opinions
concerning the Middle East political scene, there are
few observers who do not look with admiration upon the
ability of Israel to maintain a working government. Confronted by a complex of internal pressures in the midst
of a hostile external environment, it has been difficult
for many to imagine how the daily business of public services could take place.

In this study, Professor Caiden helps us understand
the nature of administration in a continuing crisis. But
his analysis goes much beyond the extraordinary circumstances of Israel's unique administrative culture.
Indeed, some aspects of that culture seem to invite comparisons with the United States. As he notes, the state
of Israel comprises persons of many cultures, social
levels and ethnic backgrounds, who should somehow be
integrated into the nation as a whole and the bureaucracy
in particular. Thus the bureaucracy must at least provide on-the-job training and devise job descriptions that
will facilitate entry and upgrade skills. In addition,
Caiden observes that Israel also suffers from the debili-
tating influences of bureaupathology. Despite the obvious differences between the two nations, repeated
parallels suggest that the Israeli experience can be
highly illuminating for students of public administration, politics and government not only in new nations,
but in the United States as well.

Professor Gerald E. Caiden, now a visiting professor
in the Graduate School of Public Affairs on the Berkeley
campus, has taught and written widely in the field of
public administration. He has taught at the London
School of Economics and Political Science, the Australian
National University at Canberra and the Hebrew University in Jerusalem. His books include the forthcoming

"Dynamics of Public Administration," to be published by Holt, Rinehart and Winston in 1971; *Administrative Reform* (Chicago: Aldine, 1969); *The Commonwealth Bureaucracy* (University of Melbourne Press, 1967); and *Career Service*, issued by the same publisher in 1965.

Since its establishment as the Bureau of Public Administration nearly 50 years ago, the Institute of Governmental Studies has maintained a continuing interest in the field of public administration, now expanded to include comparative studies on an international scale. Gerald Caiden's monograph presents a perceptive and valuable addition.

EUGENE C. LEE
Director

CHAPTER I

Introduction

The differences between societies are obvious
enough. That administrative cultures, the accepted
ways in which the members of society go about getting
things done, also differ is appreciated by any individual who has tried to do business in a foreign environment. He is made aware of differences, even though he
may know little of other behavioral patterns, institutional arrangements, communal values, cherished beliefs
or ecological responses. To convey such cultural differences to people who have been confined to their own
administrative culture requires a careful balance between
abstraction (concentration on the particular) and integration (concentration on the whole). Excursions into
the parent cultures, their resources, needs and values,
their response to innovation, and adaptation to new circumstances, are unavoidable.

Sometimes the relevance of background factors and
integrative elements is lost. The links perceived by
the observer are inadequately transmitted to his audience, and he cannot penetrate either the distorted images
projected by mass media or the bland facts contained in
official releases. New and rapidly changing societies
suffer most in this respect. They also lack both

1

extensive self-analysis and the publicity that attends the powerful.

Among the more than 50 states that have been recognized since World War II, Israel has received better than its fair share of attention from supporters and opponents alike. To supporters, it is the fulfillment of a dream, a nation reborn, an old-new land, a resurgence or renaissance of a perennial nation, a state of hope, a miracle in the desert, an eternal idea, a melting pot of nations. To opponents, it is a curse, an unwarranted intrusion on others' preserves, a David turned Goliath, an imperial aggrandizer, a capitalist tool, a harbinger of war and destruction. Amid the volume of accusations and counteraccusations, Israelis quietly go about their business of building their new state and ensuring its survival. Slowly but surely, it is overcoming its initial handicaps. There can be little doubt that, from its own viewpoint, Israel's story has been one of success, tempered here and there with failures not necessarily of its own making.

Contributing to this pattern of success and failure is Israel's administrative culture. Relatively little has been written about this culture, for reasons that will become more apparent as the analysis proceeds. But the brief career of the state of Israel provides ideal conditions for demonstrating the close identity of an administrative culture with its parent culture: its geography, ideology, societal values, economic and political systems, technology, quality of communal services, communications networks and net balance of traded resources. One can observe as well how it defines resources and obtainable goals; how it wastes and misuses resources; how it can transpose ultimate ends; and the way its institutions, ideas and activities defy the drawing of sharp boundaries.

ISRAEL SINCE INDEPENDENCE

Twenty years ago the prospect that there now would be an Israeli administrative culture to write about

looked dim. The new state would either be snuffed out at
its inception by more powerful neighbors or torn apart by
the interminable internal struggles between diverse elements. Such fears still exist, but the likelihood of
extinction is much diminished, at least for the foresee-
able future. A people that had not governed itself for
some 2000 years has demonstrated that it can revitalize
its symbols, language and folkways within a contemporary
democratic framework, while endeavoring to overcome a
legacy of dispersion and a paucity of experience in state
management. The country has continued to conduct its
business despite war and other exceptional conditions.

Geographically isolated, Israel's citizens continue
to be barred from natural intercourse across its borders.
Communications still have to be directed around hostile
neighbors who refuse to recognize Israel's existence except as a military target and reinforce its isolation
through diplomatic blackmail and economic boycott. The
natural resources of the country remain as unpromising
as ever: outside the coastal plain and river valleys,
the terrain is largely hostile, with scant and uncertain
rainfall, denuded soil cover and no important mineral
resources, except in the Dead Sea.

As socialization proceeds, the population gains
homogeneity, but diversity in race, religion, ethnicity
and culture are still prime characteristics. The early
resemblance to a vast refugee camp, as Jews from over 50
countries arrived to make new lives for themselves, has
virtually disappeared with industrialization, agricultural colonization and the growth of cities, suburbs
and new towns. But the underlying problems of peace,
economic development, social integration and assimilation, civil rights, Zionism, self-reliance and the role
of Judaism in a predominantly Jewish state, have not
been solved. They continue to plague public policy
making.

In the meantime, Israel's outlook has been transformed. It is a respected member of many international
bodies and one of the few new countries that both

receives and gives technical assistance. In several areas--language teaching, agricultural organization and research, military tactics--even older nations seek to learn from its experiences. Successful military campaigns have proven the quality and resourcefulness of the Israel Defense Forces.

There have been no attempted military coups, civil wars or revolutions, and, apart from terrorist activity, only one serious civil disturbance has taken place. Constitutionalism has been accepted by all parties, from extreme left to right. None openly advocates the overthrow of the regime by force, though some groups refuse to accept the legitimacy of the state and its rulers. In pursuit of its Zionist mission, Israel has commented on the internal affairs of other states only to protect Jews raise capital and seek immigrants.

Spectacular developments in water supply, agriculture, industry, construction and power generation have been combined with heavy defense expenditures. These developments, together with a fourfold increase in the Jewish population (excluding occupied territories) and an injection of $7 billion in foreign aid, have more than doubled the real gross national product since 1952. Exports have increased sixfold in the same period. Rapid economic growth has enabled most newcomers to free themselves from institutional dependence and to become assimilated into prevailing social patterns. The equitable distribution of wealth, at least among the Jews, has been reduced by unequal sharing in the new prosperity. Inequality, however, is still limited by high taxation, heavy public expenditures, and large-scale public and communal ownership.

The flow of immigrants has slackened dramatically, but there is no telling when it may increase again, due to persecution of Jews or the end of restrictions on Jewish emigration from other countries. By 1967, Israel was no longer a nation of immigrants: half its population had been born in the country. Since 1967, however, the occupied areas have increased fivefold the number of non-Jews subject to the Israeli government.

Israel cannot yet move in the direction of its ideal, which is more akin to the mixed welfare state of Scandinavia than to America's liberal capitalism, or the Soviet Union's centralized collectivism or the theocracy of the Vatican. Its public policies are still dominated by displaced immigrants seeking to evolve a new society based on Zionism. Twenty years is too short a time to expect much more than the consolidation of independence and the outline of the future society.

This turbulent nation lives in perpetual crisis, not knowing what is going to happen next. It has no set place in the world order; it is physically, if not psychologically, isolated from its allies and well-wishers. Its people feel themselves alone and view their predicament as unique. They are proud of their successes, gained at a high cost in human life and personal comfort, but are mindful of their many failures. They have failed to achieve those things they want above all else: security, peace and Arab recognition.

Israel includes only one-sixth of the world's Jews-- less than its stated goal--and emigration has not significantly affected the major Jewish concentrations of America, Russia, Great Britain and France. The economy suffers from speculative ventures, imbalances between sectors, price inflation, heavy adverse trade balances, some unemployment and underemployment, nagging strikes, restrictive practices and bad management.

Some immigrant groups are unable to adjust to their new homeland; integration between Jew and non-Jew has not been attempted. Infighting between small and intransigent parties has resulted in numerous political crises, causing public policy making virtually to cease and crucial decisions to be postponed. Civil liberties have been affected by broad discretionary powers under emergency laws. Social services, while technically proficient, have been most seriously affected by the diversion of resources to defense needs. Development plans, particularly decentralization, have been evaded. No one needs to be reminded of the tasks left undone and the aspirations unfulfilled.

IMPORTANCE OF ADMINISTRATIVE CULTURE

The administrative culture is only one factor that contributes to the attainment of societal objectives formulated by public policy-making processes. A society may be successful in spite of its administrative culture: its success may have been inevitable or due to external or compensatory factors, e.g., Messianic leadership. The latter, however, is most unlikely in the contemporary world, where administration is increasingly important.

In Israel's case, certain non-administrative factors are less important than they are often presumed to be. There is no proof of divine guidance, no telling what divine authority has in store for the chosen people. If Jews differ from other peoples, it is perhaps only in their ability to maintain their identity in the most adverse circumstances. The absence of abundant natural resources no longer prevents economic growth. As Singapore and Hong Kong show, this lack can be offset by good communications, cheap skilled labor and cheap power. High levels of literacy and cultural awareness are not unique to Israel, and they have dysfunctions such as endless debate, hairsplitting and undervaluation of external advice. Lack of experience in statecraft is common to all new nations though Israel was more fortunate than most in being able to call on a cadre accustomed to dealing with novel situations. The keys to success must be sought elsewhere, increasingly within the administrative culture.

Israel's administrative culture is still in the making. Nothing is settled or irrevocable, but the principal features are taking shape and hardening into a solid framework. Some traits are new and experimental, as befits a new state. Many predate the state and can be traced to the early days of the Zionist movement. A few reach further back into centuries of ghetto life: persecution, communal self-reliance, religious optimism, rootlessness and paranoia. The whole is a complex mix, a melange of varying styles drawn from many different cultural roots.

Such largesse provides a natural laboratory for administrative research. So far, few have taken advantage of this opportunity. No systematic studies of the administrative culture or any of its subsystems have been undertaken. The government of Israel has not made extensive inquiries, nor has it contracted with any other body to do so. The only officially sanctioned studies have been conducted by United Nations technical assistants: O.E. Ault (1953), F.B. Hindmarsh (1956), and O.B. Conoway (1956) all studied administrative training needs in the Israeli civil service.

Other studies have been conducted independently by the World Bank, American universities and Zionist organizations. Israeli institutions have hired overseas administrative advisers, but their studies have been limited, ad hoc, problem-centered, and in some cases confidential. Sporadic forays are undertaken by individuals attached to universities or the mass media and by specialist bodies, such as the Israel Management Association, the Israel Institute of Productivity and the Central School of Administration.

The outstanding exception to the general rule of government indifference to administrative research is the State Comptroller. This office is authorized to conduct extensive surveys into the administration of any body receiving public money--a jurisdiction that extends beyond the governmental subsystem. Other areas are covered, to a lesser extent, by the Comptrollers of the Histadrut, the Jewish Agency and other bodies including local governments, political parties, banks, insurance houses, cooperatives, youth movements and defense industries. Together with the abundant statistics available from the Central Bureau of Statistics, their surveys provide basic information from which administrative evaluations at the subsystem level could be derived.

SOME PROBLEMS OF RESEARCH

For a deeper understanding of Israel's administrative culture, a knowledge of at least four languages

(Hebrew, Arabic, English and Yiddish) is desirable. All
four, if not a sprinkling of a few more, are needed to
converse with people and to read primary sources. Without them, the researcher is at the mercy of what others
are prepared to tell or translate. This places him at a
disadvantage, for he cannot tell how much is being fil-
tered out. He also arouses instant suspicion as an outsider who may not be sympathetic, and, worse still, may
be looking for information that puts Israel in a bad
light. Linguistic knowledge indicates genuine sympathy
and understanding which is repaid by courtesy and dis-
arming frankness. Abuse of confidence, however, will
end further meaningful discourse.

The seeker of documents is likely to be disappointed
in Israel. Recordkeeping has not been a strong feature
of Israeli administration, while pre-Independence records
are scattered not only throughout Britain and Turkey, but
around the globe. Resistance movements and rebels do not
keep records or commit themselves to paper. Much has
been lost in war, fire, transit and destruction, suffer-
ing the same fate as local Jewish communities.

Good, but incomplete, collections are located in the
Israeli Government Archives and the Jewish Agency Archives
in Jerusalem. Individuals have also retained documents
in their private collections. Valiant attempts are being
made to locate, collect and centralize surviving records,
though it may already be too late to reconstruct much of
the immediate past. Habits die hard, for even today important decisions may not be formally recorded or maintained in public records.

Accessibility to persons and documents depends on
the reputation of the inquirer, the institution to which
he is attached, the purpose for which access is sought
and the use to be made of the information. If the
inquirer is unknown, formal requests are unlikely to
suffice without the help of intermediaries who are
trusted by the person or body from whom information is
sought. If the inquirer is unsuccessful, there is a
good chance that a more direct approach, at private
residences or at public and private gatherings, will

succeed. Even if access is denied, the grapevine is so
well developed that the inquirer can usually find out
what he wants to know secondhand, though there are, of
course, risks that gossip and rumor may distort the
truth.

The relatively open access to persons and information, despite threats of terrorism and spying, enables
information to flow quickly through the community. This
reduces lags in response to new challenges and improves
predictability and the ability to take immediate action.
Less time is needed for briefing, for knowledge of relevant details can be assumed. In addition, everyday contacts with the administrative culture are unavoidable,
frequent and varied. In themselves, they provide typical
illustrations of what is being repeated elsewhere.

The use of information is restricted by security,
censorship and defamation laws. Criticism, for example,
may constitute defamation if it attributes to a public
figure a criminal or hostile act or unsuitable behavior
in public office; if it harms his professional standing;
makes him subject to scorn, ridicule or hatred; or causes
others to avoid him. In practice these laws are applied
leniently, except where the security of the state is
alleged to be involved. Possibly more important is the
extent of self-censorship, a reluctance to reveal anything detrimental to the well-being of the state. This
applies not only to Israelis, but equally to outsiders
who fear either blocking future access to sources or
giving comfort to Israel's detractors.

A final inhibition is rapid change that quickly
outdates information. By the time observations have been
pieced together, the whole scene has altered and extensive revision is needed before publication. This, in
turn, cannot be completed without the writer's being left
behind again. In the meantime, the grapevine ensures
that the author's suggestions will have been incorporated
and his criticisms invalidated. This too reduces the
value of published observations. With these limitations
in mind, let us trace the evolution of Israel's administrative culture.

CHAPTER II

Sources of Administrative Culture

An administrative culture does not appear overnight or in a single generation. It develops gradually as an autonomous society marshals its resources to meet societal demands. Israel's administrative culture did not begin with the creation of the state in 1948, but can be traced back to biblical times.

BIBLICAL LAW

In parts, the Old Testament resembles an administrative manual followed by the First and Second Jewish Commonwealths. It still provides a guide and inspiration for contemporary lawmakers. There is a strong movement to return to the ways of the Book in running the modern state, less in form and content than in spirit and ethics. The accent is on justice, on public morality, respect for duly appointed authorities, compassionate administration and social equality. Bible teachings and their various interpretations by learned scholars and righteous men have been followed in Jewish communities the world over. This law was kept separate from the law of the land. The latter was subordinate to religious law in the internal affairs of the Jews, but not in their relations with non-Jews. In the territory bordering the eastern shore of the Mediterranean, the religion was preserved by remnants of Jewish communities, which continuously exchanged opinions with Diaspora Jewry. Today, this heritage is the basis of the Jewish religious law which largely governs personal relations between Jews in Israel, just as Christian, Moslem and Druze religious law govern those communities. No attempt is made to impose Jewish religious laws on non-Jews. Those most resentful of religious civil laws are not non-Jewish minorities, but the large body of Jewish non-believers and liberals.

THE OTTOMAN EMPIRE

A more modern beginning could be made with the Ottoman Empire, which imposed its style on the area for four centuries. The empire remained in power until late in World War I. By then, Zionist immigration was significant, and Arab nationalism, aided and abetted by big power rivalries, had begun to stir.

In truth, there was not much for the empire to rule. The country was largely barren and neglected. Its riches had been exploited, exhausted and abandoned. Ancient irrigation systems, vineyards, wheat fields and olive groves had reverted to desert. Towns had fallen into ruins. Centers of industry and commerce had survived, but as new centers had developed elsewhere in the Middle East they had fallen far below the level of their former glory.

Arab villagers cultivated their fields according to custom and preserved their pastures and orchards. Nomads roamed the marginal areas and came into conflict with village settlements over grazing rights. The towns served as markets and manufacturing centers. As the land was the center of three religions, the towns also served the pilgrims and protected the seminaries.

The peoples went about their business and settled their differences in their own way. The Turks were content to act as supervisors. They maintained law and order, exacted taxes, and provided essential public works for government and defense, but preferred a minimum of interference with local practices. In short, the local communities were largely self-governing, while the Ottoman administration was lax and tolerant, except when it came to enforcing imperial orders and raising troops.

BRITISH RULE

Until the British captured the country, it was a most uninviting place. Great areas of the land were desert and malarial swamp. There were no areawide services, no proper land records, no adequate police or postal systems, no telecommunication services or road and rail connections outside Jerusalem and Jaffa, no health and education systems. When the Turkish officials fled with their records, the British "found a country without a government, lacking elementary public security, ridden by poverty and disease, and handicapped by a crippled economy, primitive communications, and undeveloped social services."[1] Only in strategic terms was it an asset.

The population of less than 750,000, predominantly Arab, was totally unfit for independent self-government. There was neither strong demand for self-rule nor leadership capable of enforcing it. The people accommodated themselves to British requirements. For most, this required no change in behavior whatsoever. The nomads continued to roam the marginal areas. The agricultural settlements and villages farmed as usual in their tight-knit communities. The urban proletarian and craftsman looked for a livelihood wherever he could, while the religious seminarians and pilgrims pursued their spiritual devotions.

The British did, however, represent a break with the past. Theirs was a civilizing mission. They could not tolerate the lax standards of government to which the

---

[1] Marver H. Bernstein, *The Politics of Israel: The First Decade of Statehood* (Princeton University Press, 1957) p. 13.

local populace had become accustomed. Nor could they
stand the poverty, disease and ignorance. They drew
boundaries for the Palestinian Mandate, extended the
machinery of administration, encouraged local self-
government, and embarked on a public works program that
included public buildings, roads and railways, postal and
telecommunication services, hospitals, schools, police
stations and prisons. The injection of capital, the construction projects, the development of foreign ties, and
the substitution of more appropriate British laws for
Turkish laws--all stimulated economic activity and
attracted workers from neighboring areas.

As living standards improved, immigration and the
reduction of the death rate doubled the Arab population
in two decades. At the same time, the Jewish population
jumped as a result of growing Zionist support, European
anti-Semitism, and immigration restrictions in western
countries, which had formerly served as the main reception center for Jewish refugees and immigrants. The
British had pledged themselves to the establishment of
a Jewish national home in Palestine and could not oppose
Jewish immigration, though they could limit the influx
and restrict the land available for settlement.

The British probably underestimated Arab resentment
of continuing Jewish immigration, the resulting land
settlement and urban competition. By the time they acted
to curb further Jewish development, anti-British senti-
ment, fed by external Arab nationalist influences, was
widely evident. Restrictions on Jewish development in
turn caused Jewish hostility to the British: the continuation of restrictions during and after the Nazi Holocaust
further embittered relations. In the transformed international scene after World War II, the British could not
afford to maintain their mandate, nor were they able to
intervene between extremist Arab and Jewish factions
without being accused of bias by one side or the other.
Britain referred the problem to the United Nations, which
decided to divide the country into two states. The pre-
dominately Jewish settled areas were allotted to the
Jewish state, while Jerusalem, situated in the proposed
Arab state, was suggested as an international city.

Under the British Mandate, Arab and Jewish communities had developed along different lines. The Arabs remained unorganized outside the traditional framework, while the Jews availed themselves of every opportunity, legal and illegal, to construct a contemporary self-governing apparatus suited to eventual independence. The Jews preferred their own social services to those provided by the British, whereas the Arabs provided little for themselves and were dependent on British largesse. In the countryside, traditional Arab structures remained largely unchanged. Relations with governmental officials and neighbors were conducted through the headmen, who usually combined civil and religious duties.

The Jews persisted with their agricultural colonies run along collectivist lines, drained the swamps, planted trees, irrigated desert areas and cleared marginal land for intensive production. The colonies were attached to different political factions in the Zionist movement and were integrated into national structures.

In the towns, Arabs took advantage of British projects and expanded their own activities, while new avenues opened in the lower echelons of the British bureaucracy, particularly for Christian Arabs. The Jews also took whatever opportunities were offered by the British, for the country suffered from uncertain economic growth as well as large-scale unemployment and underemployment. Independently, the Jews constructed new towns, introduced new industries, organized their own social service systems, and built up a strong labor movement, the Histadrut, that was both self-protective and entrepreneurial.

DEVELOPMENT OF SELF-GOVERNMENT

The Arabs were cool toward the limited opportunities in local self-government provided by the British, but failed to develop national organizations among themselves or in conjunction with the Jews. In contrast, the Jews had a tradition of communal organization and the assistance of international Zionist organizations in Diaspora

Jewry. Even before the British Mandate began, they had
organized the Elected Assembly, a national legislative
body which was to be elected every three to six years.
From it was drawn the National Council, operating on a
budget raised by voluntary taxation. The National Council selected the National Council Executive, which received official recognition from the British despite
opposition by ultra-orthodox Jews and disputes within the
Mandate authorities. The jurisdiction of the National
Council Executive covered internal political disputes,
labor problems and later, social services. In order to
develop a Jewish national home, the Mandate had accepted
the need for a consultative body drawn from the Zionist
movement. It appointed first the Zionist Organization
and then, in 1929, the Jewish Agency. With jurisdiction
over immigration, settlement and economic development,
the Jewish Agency in time became more important than the
National Council: by 1948 it had become virtually a provisional government. Thus, when the British withdrew,
dismantling the machinery of government as they went, the
Arabs were unprepared for independent self-government,
whereas the Jews could reorganize their institutions into
a modern bureaucratic state.

As it happened, an independent Arab state never came
into existence. Along with many Arab notables in Palestine, the neighboring Arab states were bitterly opposed
to the establishment of an independent Jewish state in
the region and urged the Arabs not to cooperate with the
autonomous Jewish institutions and to resist the formation of a sovereign state of Israel. Warfare broke out
soon after the partition plan became known and continued
throughout the hasty British withdrawal. The National
Council and the Jewish Agency formed a Joint Emergency
Committee to plan for independence and to constitute a
provisional government.

At the termination of the British Mandate, a 37-
member Provisional Council of State (comprised of 14
members of the 42-member National Council, 11 members of
the Jewish Agency Executive, and 12 others drawn from
political parties and communities not represented in the
other bodies) proclaimed the existence of the new State,

Israel. It elected 13 Ministers from the council to be
the Provisional Government, and two days later elected a
President, who became its 38th member. The Council of
State was the legislature until proper elections could be
held. The Provisional Government reconstructed 17 ministries from the remnants of over 40 different departments
of the British Administration of Palestine, and an equal
number of departments formerly administered by the Jewish
Agency and the National Council Executive.

The new nation had already been invaded by its immediate neighbors, but the state of active war was ended
first by cease-fires and then by an armistice. According
to the terms of the armistice, the cease-fire lines became the temporary boundaries pending final settlement.
Israel had increased its territory beyond the boundaries
provisionally proposed by the United Nations Partition
Plan. The remainder, which was supposed to have become
an independent Arab state, was annexed by Jordan or
assumed by Egypt. The large number of Arabs who had left
the areas allocated to the new Jewish state or acquired
by Israel in the fighting, were unable to return. Their
places were taken by the large influx of Jewish refugees
from Europe and from Islamic countries, where their position had become precarious as a result of the Arab set-
back. By 1952 the Arab population was dwarfed by that of
the Jews, whose numbers had doubled in four years.

This was a period of acute hardship and travail
for all concerned, forever etched in the memory of those
who experienced the trauma, drama and chaos of those
disorganized years. Pre-Independence governmental
arrangements--laws, legal system, local government, etc.-
continued in force, except for laws specially prepared by
the Provisional Government for Independence. Administrative methods and procedures were also adopted piecemeal
and adapted to the new conditions. Thus the standardization and uniformity of the British Mandate soon disappeared. Long standing British practices existed side by
side with haphazard impromptu arrangements adopted by
inexperienced party functionaries under the stress of
war. These were later supplemented by inexperienced

newcomers recreating administrative practices from their countries of origin. Not until the initial dislocation was overcome could it be said that an Israeli administrative culture had come into being.

By that time, the Jewish settlement founded on political Zionism had experienced 60 years of progress and had grown accustomed to acting independently. External contacts had been firmly established throughout the world. National ideology and leadership existed. Settlements had been strategically located and consolidated. Large towns were thriving centers of commerce and industry; small towns were useful marketing centers and coordinating points. Hamlets were capable of self-defense. Institutions capable of implementing statehood were linked both formally and informally.

The 1948-49 war had brought death and destruction, but it had also taught self-reliance and had given the people pride and determination that were essential to surmount the difficulties accompanying the mass influx of Jewish refugees. Food, clothing and accommodation were still scarce; unemployment was rife; and living standards had declined sharply. The new State of Israel was sorely tried, but weathered the period, although not without scars. The pre-Independence ideology had to be adapted to immediate problems: to the changed geographical context, to non-Zionist immigration, to problems of assimilation and to the unexpected numbers of new settlers.

FOUR STRANDS OF ADMINISTRATIVE CULTURE

As a result of these developments, Israel's administrative culture combines at least four different strands. First, at local levels there is the indigenous Middle Eastern style. This is found particularly in Arab areas, which, though changing with the rest of the Middle East, remain substantially unaltered. Business is transacted at a regal pace, in a charmingly courteous, if exasperating, fashion. Traditional institutions place a premium

on deference to authority and status, bargaining skills
and displays of bureaucratic officiousness. Rank is
highly esteemed, and there is a wide gap in rewards and
perquisites between top and bottom, just as there is between those with authority and those without. This styl
is similar in many respects to Jewish ghetto methods of
settling internal matters and dealing with outside
authority. It is a bargaining rather than a bureaucrati
posture.

Second, the British legacy lingers in important
areas of national government, despite attempts to reduce
its influence in the early days of the state. The
British pattern is still discernible in the legal system
in police organization; in post office, customs and rail
ways administration; and, to a lesser extent, in local
government, public utilities, banking and port control.
It is a no-nonsense, orderly, condescending, bureaucrati
approach, with little room for bargaining, local initiative or disruption.

The third strand is composed of traditions brought
by Jewish immigrants from their countries of origin, as
varied as the contents of a spicery. Paranoiac ghetto
attitudes mingle with dynamic, cosmopolitan, liberal entrepreneurship. Efficient, dogmatic, Central European
bureaucrats work alongside contemplative philosophers
unused to standardization and impersonal legal-rational
authority. These variations are contained within a
framework of bureaucratization, professionalism, functional requirements and clientele pressures. While in
time they lose some of their sharpness, they do create
a continuing problem in cooperation and coordination.
Occasionally, under pressure, they explode into conflict

The fourth strand--the *vatiquim* (or old timers) and
their native-born offspring--embraces a similar variety
of styles related to position, experience, education,
age, political ideology and personal ambitions. Labor
Zionist pioneers, skilled in political infighting and
insurgency tactics, affirm their inherent visionary
powers, their pragmatic "feel" of things, and their

confidential, in-group decisionmaking. Middle class
sabras (native-born Israelis) fresh out of military service or the university, however, look to American models
whenever they can.

Any distinctiveness about the Israeli administrative
culture is due primarily to the fourth strand. The elder
members consciously or unconsciously, have achieved pre-
eminence in most walks of life and have sought to impose
their style and values. They dislike the Middle Eastern
style, but are prepared to tolerate it, believing that
sooner or later its obvious inferiority will be its own
downfall. Moreover, they are adept at using the Middle
Eastern style and, being hard bargainers themselves,
understand the nuances of personal confrontation. The
younger generations, both Jewish and non-Jewish, are more
resentful; they refuse to learn the rules of the Middle
Eastern game, preferring more bureaucratic and impersonal
modes of conduct.

The elderly have a love-hate relationship toward
the British heritage: they want to rid the country
of British influence, but they retain a sneaking affec-
tion for its better points. Again, the younger generations, which barely remember the British, are less sympathetic to British civility, but greatly impressed by
American know-how. Both young and old hope that the
third immigrant strand will end once newcomers are thor-
oughly integrated and absorbed in the *sabra* culture. In
fact, the settlers' own styles may owe more to the other
three influences than they would admit, and they themselves may have been doing some of the assimilating. The
evolving administrative style is a peculiar mix, and,
depending on the opposite party, skilled administrators
switch from one approach to another, adopting that stance
that promises the best results. The ease of transition
is disconcerting to outsiders, who expect a standard
stereotype, only to be confronted with representatives
who seem to find themselves at home anywhere and able to
reach a common level of understanding with anyone.

CHAPTER III

Context of the Administrative Culture

The mixture of diverse administrative styles will
probably remain an important feature of Israel's administrative culture for some generations, even longer if
Israel continues to attract immigrants from around the
world. But it is not the most important trait inherited
from pre-Independence circumstances. The years 1948-
1952, exceptional though they were, did not represent a
complete break with the past.

Even when Israeli leaders had the chance to start
afresh, they preferred to stick with the familiar and
well-tried, to adapt what already existed to new conditions. The Basic Laws, which will eventually become the
Constitution, bear a striking resemblance to those of
Jewish self-governing institutions before Independence.
The underground defense forces, combined with remnants
of irregular forces, were organized into the Israel
Defense Force. The Jewish Agency and the Histadrut were
not abolished: the former was reduced in status, but the
latter plays an enhanced economic role. The numerous political parties resisted any attempt to construct a depoliticized civil administration. The continuation of so
many pre-Independence institutions, the longevity of
leaders in public office, and the persistence of dominant
societal values, all ensure the preservation of many

elements of the administrative culture adopted by the Jews under the British Mandate.

For the Jewish community, life under the Mandate was precarious and often fraught with danger. Rapport with the British and the Arabs fluctuated widely, but over the long run, relations with both groups deteriorated. Authorities could not always be relied upon to enforce law and order or to administer justice fairly. The variable flow of Jewish funds and immigrants, the lack of local capital, limited markets, crop failures and disease all contributed to low productivity, economic depression and high seasonal unemployment. Illegal immigration, arms supplies, and military training caused external hostility, while internally the Jewish community was rent by deep religious and ideological disputes.

To cope with this situation, the "key system" was used in filling public offices. Each party or group was allotted positions according to its votes at the polls; each had a stake in and a commitment to the system; each was able to share the spoils. In public debate, some semblance of unity was ensured by adherence to Zionist pioneering ideals and by the need for self-defense in the face of common dangers.

Much decisionmaking was carried on in private, through close personal relationships and informal communications. This was particularly true of conspiratorial activities. There was much reliance on trust and on the pragmatic mode of operations, which was also demanded by coalition maintenance. Improvisation was the order of the day. The price of failure was high; the penalties imposed by the community severe. Long after the formation of the State of Israel, its leaders did not alter this pattern. But then, the nature of their problems had not really changed.

CRISIS ATMOSPHERE

Israeli administration is conducted under crisis conditions. Though continuous improvement has been recorded, the situation remains precarious and fraught with danger. The State of Israel has been subject to such an unending series of blows that its people have learned to accept bad news as a matter of course without panic. Nobody can predict when or where the next blow will fall, but most expect extraordinary events to occur The breathing space between crises is short; the pressures rarely diminish; the problems do not seem to change. Security remains elusive. The policies of hostile neighbors are not consistent; terrorism is not structured. Nor are the policies of professed allies consistent, which makes the supply of foreign arms uncertain.

Incessant conflict, unless compensated by achievement, reduces morale as the death toll rises and costs mount. The present is heavily mortgaged to ensure a future. The country is deeply in debt: per capita national debt is the highest in the world. Inflation and devaluation are part of the price of survival. So too is the intense competition for scarce resources that leads to administrative penny pinching, inability to replace depreciated capital and extensive fund-raising abroad. The foregone alternatives cannot be measured in terms of reduced standards of living and underdeveloped social services alone, for consideration must also be given to cumulative effects and psychological repercussions.

The diversion of resources has reduced the capacity to absorb and integrate newcomers. The State of Israel, however, has pledged itself to an open door policy for all Jews who want to settle in the homeland. In the absence of a quota system or other restrictions, the flow of immigrants depends on the intensity of anti-Semitism elsewhere, the willingness of foreign governments to allow Jews to emigrate, and the success of Zionist propaganda. Each immigrant family must be transported, provided with facilities and accommodations and helped to assimilate into the new culture, irrespective of personal circumstances. In turn, citizens have to learn to accept the newcomers as equals.

Solutions to these serious problems require some measure of consensus within the society. They demand binding agreements between diverse political factions, which have so far shown no willingness to merge their identities in larger political organizations of roughly the same persuasion. Like other new states, Israel--under less favorable conditions--is expected to compress into a generation what older states achieved in many generations.

The persistent presence of compelling problems in an atmosphere of crisis produces a hand-to-mouth administrative existence. Attention is concentrated on the immediate present. Concern for the future is limited; it is enough to live through the current crisis. Just standing still entails a struggle to maintain existing resources and to ward off cuts and encroachments.

Though time perspectives tend to be short, the heavy strain of administration requires a high level of personal devotion and self-sacrifice, which is maintained by idealism and romantic dreams about the future. The aim is to fight off each crisis in such a way that the dreams seem that much nearer to realization. Standing still is the lowest achievement; success is measured by progress. To progress one has to keep up with leaders who are forever pushing ahead, never content to remain quiescent. Deterioration or decline is morally repulsive: it is the acknowledged sign, not just of failure, but of a societal dropout who has given up or fallen too far behind to be able to catch up again. Such a person is to be pitied, but not rehabilitated.

The pace of action is therefore very fast, very compelling. Relaxation is an expensive luxury. There is too much to be done, too little time and too few people available or able to get on with the essential tasks. Formal processing takes too long. Better, then, to rely on people one knows and trusts, people who think along the same lines, people who can be depended upon at all times to do their best.

Insecurity, despite its dysfunctions, presents a stimulus. When existence is imperiled, everything else becomes secondary; there is no alternative, no choice but to help one another whatever the odds. The persistence of an external threat of annihilation, following the actual annihilation of one-third of the world's Jews has united all the Jews in Israel. The threat brings out the best in them--creativity, discipline, comradeship and resolve--and enables them to tackle the seemingly impossible.

The struggle for survival is heroic. How long it can be maintained is still to be seen, but three factors reinforce its intensity: (a) the long history of persecution in the Diaspora, (b) the fear of assimilation and the loss of distinctiveness if Jews have no homeland where they can develop freely, and (c) the belief that no one will come to Israel's rescue if it does not stand up for itself.

In their lifetime enough Israelis have seen swift changes of attitude towards them to make them paranoiacally suspicious of fair-weather friends.

Success has bred self-confidence. What has been done before can be done again and improved upon. Israelis begin with the assumption of success: they do not anticipate failure. This makes them appear excessively self-confident and even cocksure, but it is mere bravado, to avoid the contemplation of defeat and disaster that might undermine confidence and create panic. It covers the obvious truth that failure means the end of all their dreams--the Third Jewish Commonwealth, the Jewish homeland in Palestine, Zionism, Jewish self-respect--and a return to the status of the wandering Jew who, in the past, has had to move on every second or third generation, unable to capitalize on past effort.

SECURITY MEASURES AND THEIR RESULTS

Security needs have been more directly instrumental in promoting successful policy performance. It is well

known that defense expenditures stimulate the economy,
present multipurpose investment opportunities, provide
employment, socialize young people, develop administrators and do much more in non-military directions. (All
of this could probably be achieved as readily if the
money were spent directly on such purposes.) Modern warfare requires a highly sophisticated economy, a well-
trained people, a rapidly improving technology and a
swift transformation from peace to war. Military investments have multiplier effects: they serve many purposes
and stimulate research and creativity. Military strategy requires uneconomic investments, risk-taking and improvisation as well as planning, abundant reserves and
coordinated logistics. Military strength reassures
overseas investors and traders, appeals to armament producers and has heartening effects on national morale.
In short, militarism backed by centuries of persecution,
emphasizes collectivism, communal norms, concepts of
unity and other-regarding. This effect offsets to a
large extent the individualism, the ideological fission
and the voluntarism that might otherwise fragment the
population and prevent cooperation.

ZIONISM

The pioneering, goal-directed ideology of Zionism
unifies both the people and the leadership in a manner
second only to the threat of military annihilation. A
distinction, however, should be made between Zionist
ideology and the Zionist movement. Ever since the dispersion of the Jews following the destruction of the
Second Temple (about 70 A.D.), Jewish prayers have reflected a longing to return and rebuild the homeland
that God had promised to them. The idea of return, the
core of Zionism, remained a dream until the nineteenth
century. At that time, with the permission of the
Turkish rulers, Jews took active steps to settle in the
Promised Land, on either a self-financed or a subsidized
basis. Unlike the existing Jewish settlers, these Jews
came not solely for religious activities, but also to
gain a self-supporting livelihood.

The idea grew from settlement to colonization to
national homeland to national state, i.e., an independent sovereign state open to all Diaspora Jewry and
aimed at the resurgence of Jewish culture in a free
society. The Zionist movement split over how to attain
this ideal and has since remained divided into many
small, competing factions. Each faction is a political
movement in its own right, wedded to the others only by
the establishment of the Third Jewish Commonwealth.
The movement has long suffered from diffusion of authority, excessive partisanship, poor central housekeeping
and inadequate financial control and accounting--traits
it bequeathed to the new state.

Within Israel, local politics came to be dominated
by the Second Aliyah (wave) of immigrants, mainly Jews
from Russia. They arrived in the decade before World
War I, espousing collectivism, land colonization, self-
reliance and Hebraicism. They saw themselves as the
vanguard of Judaism, prepared to make sacrifices to
restore the Third Jewish Commonwealth. This self-image
of the select of Jewry laying the foundations of the new
millenium still looms over public policy making. Member
of this elite--latter day visionaries and prophets--*know*
they are right. Only those who are making similar sacri
fices and bearing similar responsibilities for public
policy making, they claim, have the right to criticize.
No one else really knows or understands Israeli society
as they do, and as evidence they point to their repeated
confounding of outside experts and critics. They form
the oldest political elite in the world, an elite that
has experienced much, including the traumas of emigratio
and the uncertainties of four wars. They have shown
exceptional personal courage and fortitude and they have
made major personal sacrifices for comparatively low pub
lic rewards.

Hagiography is excusable in testifying to the excep
tional character of the leaders who made the Zionist
movement so successful. They were products of an emanci
pated Central European Jewish intelligentsia subsequentl
wiped out by the Holocaust and Communist imperialism.

It has nevertheless contributed much to European Communist and Socialist parties and to social movements in both North America and the British Commonwealth.[1] They shared the same

> two apparently contradictory yet complementary mental attitudes: on the one hand, limitless ambitions, apocalyptic, chiliastic and utopian thinking, often of the crudest kind; on the other, a cramping absorption in pettifogging details, coupled with hysterical fears of weakness and incompetence.[2]

Every Zionist leader has had to fight his way through the thicket of Zionist politics and to demonstrate his capacity to get results. Penalties for failure have been severe. The end product has been a group of leaders with a marked capacity to govern while demonstrating

> ability to recognize needs...inner compulsion to act in the public interest...receptivity to new ideas... ability to set challenging and realistic goals...ability to integrate plans, ideas, programs and operations in a rational whole.[3]

---

[1] A brief summary of the background of the emancipated Jewish intelligentsia is found in V.S. Frank, "Lenin and the Russian Intelligentsia," in Leonard Schapiro and Peter Reddaway, eds., *Lenin: The Man, the Theorist, the Leader* (New York: Praeger, 1967), pp. 23-36.

[2] John Keep, "Lenin as Tactician," ibid., pp. 135-158. See p. 138.

[3] G.A. Graham, *America's Capacity to Govern* (University of Alabama Press, 1960).

Despite the influx of non-Zionists and the disillusionment of some Zionists, most Israelis agree with their leaders that there is nowhere else for Jews to live a full and free life. They sympathize with Jews who are prohibited from migrating, but they hold no brief for Diaspora Jews who are free to migrate but stay where they are, and they positively resent the emigrants from Israel. They are prepared to shoulder heavy burdens and to sacrifice themselves if need be, for the sake of a better life for their children. The future is what counts, and they believe that history will one day recognize their unswerving dedication to the regeneration of a distinguished nation.

Proud of their accomplishments, they delight in displaying the results, in letting their thought and effort speak for themselves. They drive themselves to the full, always looking for something to do, restless, resourceful, stubborn; they have little time for trivia, elaborateness or genteel living. Perhaps very little of this is attributable to Zionist ideology rather than to other social drives, but the results tend in the same direction.

Loyalty to Zionism is combined with flexibility in objectives, long, medium and short-term. There is a kind of opportunistic dogmatism, geared to the immediate reality but fixed on the ultimate ideal, justifying a variety of actions and numerous twists and turns in strategy. Being goal-oriented, rather than consensus-maintaining, the administrative culture can innovate, restructure itself, substitute new goals when others have been fulfilled and generally evolve spontaneously. Because of persistent crisis, however, it must also both react to new problems as they arise and maintain harmony between divergent interests, lest important segments break down.

EXTERNAL AID

The Zionist movement outside Israel has been a considerable help in promoting support and raising funds for the new state, but it has not been the sole source of help. Israel has been aided at various times by the Communist bloc, the United States, France and West Germany. Several small European states, victims of Nazi occupation, have gone beyond technical assistance, loans, arms sales and cultural exchanges: they have made a moral commitment unusual in international politics without some *quid pro quo*.

Except for gifts and reparations, Israel has insisted on paying for most goods received and has not sought privileged treatment from international bodies. External purchases have been made possible by high domestic taxation and by loans and grants made by Diaspora Jewry as permitted by their governments. Much effort is required to maintain enthusiasm for donations to a country that many donors may never see. Then too, donors may disagree with or accord low priority to the purposes for which their donations are used. Offers cannot be refused, although they may create problems. Donors may meet capital costs of a project but not the high operating costs; or they may build houses but not provide the furniture. When recipients depend on the generosity of donors, planning becomes a nightmare. Nevertheless, it is comforting for a country to have such support, particularly in emergencies.

DEFICIENCIES IN STAFFING

The benefits of external aid have not been felt in staffing. Israel has not attracted the talent and experience needed to run large-scale enterprises nor has it been able to provide itself with adequately trained manpower. While the nation has a surfeit of small shopkeepers and craftsmen, it is seriously deficient in professionals, highly skilled workers in modern trades and in management personnel.

The educational system, particularly the institutes of higher education, have had a pedagogic rather than vocational emphasis. Their graduates have not always been able to find a niche in Israeli society, yet

training is not available in many important areas.
Except for language instruction, newcomers have had to
find their own way in the labor market, since opportunities for adult education and retraining have been rather
limited. Many compete for prestige employment that does
not always go to the most deserving, while low status
jobs are filled by ill-equipped workers. In these respects, Israel hardly differs from other societies, except perhaps in the degree of mismatching of needs and
talents.

More serious problems exist in abundance. First is
the large proportion of "passengers," i.e., people of
work age who are either unable to function at all, or
are unable to perform the tasks they are supposed to do.
The passengers are carried along by everyone else.
Second, the egalitarian pre-Independence labor philosoph
of "jack-of-all-trades-and-master-of-none" persists, fos
tered by collective and cooperative organizations and by
protective trade unions. Third, there is little appre-
ciation of the new types of expertise and specialization
required by contemporary society, because academic learn
ing, religious knowledge and the older professions continue to command greater respect. Fourth, despite the
ease of travel, the work force is relatively immobile as
a result of security rules, compressed salary differen-
tials, high progressive income taxes, restrictive labor
practices and sheer reluctance to branch into something
new. Fifth, the labor market is distorted by defense
needs. Sixth, many newcomers are unable to adapt to
their new environment. Finally, the rapid expansion in
the numbers of administrative positions has caused them
to be filled by inexperienced, unqualified and ineffi-
cient persons who cannot be dismissed or replaced.

Despite all these problems, however, the state has
muddled through. Things have been done, after a fashion
with enthusiasm, improvisation and devotion substituting
for skill. The evenness and quality of standards have
left much to be desired. Business administration has
been one of the worst performers, while agricultural

enterprise has been one of the most successful. Like-
wise, the performance of the Israel Defense Force has
been creditable, but both the Jewish Agency and the
Histadrut empire have been failing the society. Naturally, those institutions that require external aid
the most are the ones that have failed to recognize
their need. Though the disparities have tended to widen,
and demands for rectification have grown, the response
by Israel's leaders has been poor.

THE STATUS OF ADMINISTRATION

The downgrading of administration by the elite is
readily explainable. The Israeli national image is
that of a farmer or artisan or soldier, not an office
worker or salesman. Pioneer values emphasize the doer,
the man of physical action, not the middle man or the
boss. This, of course, is a reaction against both the
life of the ghetto and the traditional role of the Jew
in the Diaspora. In addition, administrative arts are
supposed to be second nature; they need no learning,
for anyone can perform them. Finally, before 1948, few
people in Israel realized what was really involved in
administration. More attention has been paid since,
but the status of administrative study in academic cir-
cles was low until relatively recently, despite the
obvious need to improve the general quality of administrative performance. One does not go far in Israel
without hearing the word *balagun*, a local term for a
muddle, reminiscent of the chaos of early independence.

Popular dissatisfaction with administrative performance is a debating topic that never fails to arouse
interest. Everybody seems to have his pet anecdote and
further ammunition is readily available in the daily
press. Visitors cannot help being impressed by the incessant debate over the administrative culture. Government and labor administration are particularly favored
targets, presumably because they are the best known and
the most open. However, an opinion survey in 1967 among
first year undergraduates studying public administration

showed understanding of both good and bad points. Many
of these students had worked for short periods in government administration. While general complaints and
adverse images were reflected, the students' answers
tended to approximate reality. The evidence suggests
that most people have a built-in bias against administration; that bad memories of past administration coupled
with recurrent shortcomings perpetuate the adverse image;
that there is little expectation that things will soon
improve, or that anyone will act on complaints; and that
there is no real pressure for drastic administrative
reforms. It may well be that performance is bad. Alternatively, expectations may be unrealistic and beyond
fulfillment, and the general public, reviewing the
administrative culture from the viewpoint of clientele
needs, may fail to take into consideration all the
demands placed upon it.

POPULAR ASPIRATIONS

Tolerance of maladministration contrasts with the
high aspirations of Zionists for Israel and of Israeli
citizens for themselves. Israelis demand much of themselves. They want to better the *goyim*, the non-Jews,
not to prove racial superiority, but to rebel against
past repression, past mistakes, past defenselessness,
and past rootlessness. It is a rebellion against bondage. They turn their backs on the immediate past and
seek emancipation in high aspirations, in self-
identification with communal successes. Their aspirations differ little from those of men the world over:
peace, privacy, high living standards, freedom of
personal expression, good social services and education,
equal opportunity, mutual tolerance. They do not wait
for miracles. They realize that only hard work can
realize their goals, with everyone making his contribution as best he can. But they do not yet fully appreciate that there are certain areas, including administration, where good intentions alone are not enough;
that uncoordinated individual efforts may compound the
very mistakes that everyone is trying to avoid.

In recent years, values and standards have been changing. After generations of deprivation, Israelis want to be more self-indulgent; they are beginning to demand better services and a wider choice of products. They are no longer content to take what is offered. They are more discriminating, and with a higher standard of living they can begin to pick and choose. They are growing tired of emphasis on a future that never comes, while life ebbs away in discomfort. They want more *now*, though they are still prepared to shoulder extra burdens if the need is obvious (as it is from the standpoint of security).

There is increased awareness, too, that rising expectations have to be met before the dissatisfaction of the disadvantaged explodes into civil disorder. Growth provides more opportunity for self-indulgence, but it remains to be seen how much response there will be to the concept of service. In the meantime, uninfluential people are still imposed upon, restricted in their choices, brushed aside in decisionmaking, abused by bureaucrats and kept uninformed about matters directly concerning them.

SUMMARY

Israel's administrative legacy can be summarized as having the following characteristics: (1) crisis atmosphere; (2) plethora of compelling problems requiring immediate action; (3) heavy security burden; (4) goal-oriented pioneering ideology; (5) capable leadership backed by a determined people; (6) external aid; (7) staffing deficiencies; (8) low valuation of administration; and (9) high aspirations. Repeated reference will be made to these characteristics in analyzing the evolving administrative culture, though some receive more detailed examination than others. Additional characteristics have become more pronounced since the creation of the state of Israel, though these too can often be traced back to the pre-Independence administrative culture. The distinction is one of emphasis only.

CHAPTER IV

A Pre-Bureaucratic Society

Israel is an organizational society with strong tendencies toward bureaucratization derived from Europe, but it is not yet a truly bureaucratic society. Though its administrative subsystems are well differentiated and formally separated, they are so interrelated that the informal operations of one subsystem cannot be treated in isolation from the others. In a bureaucratic society, the predominant form of social combination is the bureaucracy; major social problems are tackled through bureaucratic mechanisms. Bureaucracies deal with defined problems; their innovating elites direct social activities through formal rules. But in Israel the entire citizenry is not yet organized bureaucratically. Not all social activities are conducted through bureaucratic mechanisms; bureaucratic problem-solving is not accepted by all citizens. Israelis are not yet a bureaucratic people.

NON-BUREAUCRATIZED GROUPS

While most Israelis accept the bureaucratic system, certain groups do not. As in days of old, the Bedouin still roam parts of Sinai, the Negev, Samaria and

Galilee. They confine themselves largely to their own company, keeping their contact with bureaucracies to a minimum. Save for the occasional governmental check, they are left alone. In addition, religious extremists, except those organized from outside, prefer to isolate themselves and minimize their contacts with external groups. Even though their numbers are small, they represent a significant proportion of the population.

Other Jewish and non-Jewish Middle Easterners who are unable to adapt themselves to a bureaucratic society are also left largely alone, but compared to the Bedouin, they receive a higher level of attention and more assistance. The young people in these communities are more inclined to accept bureaucratization and move away from the older society.

Since 1967, the government has not attempted to impose bureaucratic organization in those newly administered territories where it had not existed previously. However, bureaucrats themselves have started to move in this direction. Their sense of professionalism has joined with personal responsibility and social compassion. Just as officials went out of their way to aid the assimilation of Jewish newcomers in the early years of nationhood, so they have started to teach the norms of behavior in a bureaucratic society to those who now seek their assistance. At present, this is limited to elementary details such as completing forms and queuing. Further bureaucratization awaits political decisions about the future of the administered territories.

NON-BUREAUCRATIZED ACTIVITIES

The amount of self-help and voluntary activity cannot be determined accurately. The number of voluntary societies suggests that non-bureaucratized activities are still important in Israel, but as the population grows and people become more accustomed to the system, the bureaucracy takes over. This has been the tendency in religious and cultural activities, as well as in other spheres. The collective agricultural settlements and some of the smaller Histadrut cooperatives were originally conceived as non-bureaucratic activities. But they have become increasingly bureaucratized, although a few still try to preserve their ideological dissent.

In agriculture, the private cooperative *moshav* has overtaken the communal *kibbutz* as the numerically predominant form of Jewish rural settlement, but it is facing serious structural problems. The *moshav's* basic size is too small for modern capital-intensive production and it is not able to industrialize like the *kibbutz*. National planning has forced a measure of bureaucratic organization on both agricultural forms, particularly on the larger units with professional management, hired labor, factories and regional schools. Nonetheless, the continued emphasis on self-help, job rotation, self-government, collective decisionmaking and unstructured social activities means that they are less bureaucratized than private property farmed by tenants or hired laborers working for a landlord.

About half of all industrial establishments are proprietorships; another 20 percent are partnerships; and together they employ over one-quarter of all job holders. In 1960-1961, 21.1 percent of all employed persons worked in firms with less than 10 employees. Thirty percent were in those employing from 10 to 50 persons. The size of the average establishment is increasing, with the most significant growth among the largest. In 1955, 24.2 percent of the non-agricultural labor force was employed in establishments with less than 10 persons, 59.9 percent in those with less than 50 persons, and only 10.5 percent in establishments employing over 300. By 1965, the latter figure had risen to 18.5 percent. But the average size of businesses dealing with clothing, wood, leather and metal products, machinery, mining and quarrying was still less than 10 persons. Israel remains the land of small-scale businesses whose political pressure retards the deepening bureaucratization of Israeli society.

NON-BUREAUCRATIC MORES

Many Israelis cannot accept the philosophical basis of a bureaucratic society. They do not like being organized or told what to do under threat of bureaucratic sanctions. They are individualists who resent "big brother," be he governmental authority, paternal capitalist, protective union or altruistic foreigner. They retain the legacy of the ghetto, of persecution, rootlessness, autocracy, deprivation and insecurity.

They do not take kindly to elitism although they tend to be elitist. If one Jew is as good as another, he is better than the Gentile. If one Zionist is as good as another, he is better than the assimilated Jew. If one Israeli is as good as another, he is better than the *yo'ordim* (emigrants).

Nevertheless, the ethos is egalitarian. Equality of sacrifice entails equality of respect. Egalitarianism is institutionalized in cooperatives and collectives, in voluntarism, in national ideology, in social mores, economic rewards and political policy. Jews are not to be exploited by fellow Jews--or by anyone else in their homeland. Each new wave of settlers is to be accorded fair treatment and equal opportunity; failure to meet expectations reinforces demands for equal consideration. Egalitarianism is expressed in speech, dress, entertaining, taxation, salaries, housing and communal facilities. It is apparent also in the treatment of women and in general resentment of anybody who, for no good reason, considers himself superior. It largely governs the labor movement and helps non-Jewish workers attain equal rights.

Consequently, bureaucratic elites cannot rely on status and rank alone, nor can they assume obedience and compliance. On the contrary, subordinates resent bureaucratic discipline; they show their reluctance to accept authority by questioning instruction, by passive resistance and often by resorting to strikes against the advice of their own leaders.

The opponents of bureaucratism are losing out.
They have managed to retain their influence because
of their entrenchment in certain key political and
administrative positions. They are supported by those
who reject the bureaucratic society, by those who have
suffered at the hands of autocratic bureaucracies both
in their countries of origin and in Palestine, and by
those who feel that they suffer discrimination at the
hands of Israeli bureaucrats. But time is not on their
side. The old guard will eventually die out. New
generations, fully integrated and knowing no other society, will accept bureaucratic mores and operate bureaucracies whose efficacy is now evident.

The scale of organizations is expanding, society
is more differentiated and structured, professionalism
is spreading. Past excesses are being eradicated and
safeguards against abuse have been strengthened. Bureaucratization per se is no longer opposed except by
isolated critics. Well run bureaucracies are accepted,
even admired. Isrealis are jealous of the ease with
which more advanced countries run their organizational
societies. They point with pride to the Israel Defense
Forces and the airline El Al, both notably proficient
organizations, and look forward to the day when other
bureaucracies perform as well.

BUREAUPATHOLOGY

It is not bureaucratism that is feared, but the
bureaupathology that has accompanied it in Israel. Some
of the oldest institutions in the Jewish community--the
Jewish Agency, Histadrut, political parties, governmental
agencies--are the worst offenders. Some sections are so
bad that reformers would prefer to dismember them and
start again rather than simply reconstruct and remodel.
Even allowing for exaggeration and distortion, the extent
of bureaupathology is too great to be tolerated.

The symptoms include the rate at which the best
products of society seek other careers. Administrative

activities have inadequate resources, and bureaucrats make do with unsuitable accommodations, poor equipment and depressing work conditions. The bureaucrat--the *pakid*--is a figure of fun, demoralized by hostile criticism, hardpressed, overstrained and underpaid. He lacks incentives for better work performance and is seemingly unaware of the concept of service. Many have been thrust into positions beyond their abilities. Personal deficiencies are not corrected, for there are not enough training programs, qualified instructors, funds or social incentives.

Scientific management is largely unknown in many of the older institutions. It certainly is not practiced, although it may receive lip service for public relations purposes. As a result, these institutions rely on non-bureaucratic modes of administrative behavior and adopt the most complex bureaucratic procedures. From the inside they do not appear bureaucratic enough: they seem too inconsistent, unsystematic, unorganized, unprofessional and confused. But from the outside they appear too bureaucratic, too rigid, circumlocutory, cold, defensive, uncaring and superior.

There are no simple remedies for bureaupathology. The achievement of peace would help, as would increased capital investment, large-scale training programs, work incentives and lower direct taxes. But none of these can be had for the asking. It will take even longer to overcome such attitudes as inability to cope with bureaucratic ritual, the need to personalize business relationships, impatience stemming from delayed goal gratification and narrowness of vision.

Currently, the problem is being attacked on many fronts. Middle managers and potential policy makers are being sent abroad for training and overseas experts are being sought for temporary assignments. Agencies such as the Israel Management Association and the Israel Institute of Productivity are trying to create a climate conducive to scientific management. In conjunction with academic and training institutions, they are extending research and teaching in scientific methods. Experienced administrators in highly reputable organizations, particularly the Israel Defense Force, are being transferred to ailing organizations with a carte blanche to put things right. Small enterprises are being consolidated and rationalized into large entities. Native born *sabras* are gradually replacing immigrants in middle and senior administration ranks.

Such processes, however, cannot be hurried. The bureaucratic malaise is deeply rooted; attempts to prune its shoots have sometimes strengthened underground resistance and provoked tough defensive measures. So far, the skirmishes have been minor. The hardest battles will be fought in the next decade, when the *sabra* generation takes control over public policy making and management.

CHAPTER V

Policy Formation

Israel is a highly politicized country. At least 85 percent of those eligible to vote do so at national elections, and many of these are party members. Politics is taken very seriously. Interest is reflected in the relatively large number of politically oriented newspapers and in the amount of space they devote to political reporting. Since Independence, however, partisanship has probably declined. People are now prepared to switch allegiances and to view programs and platforms more impartially.

PRE-INDEPENDENCE PATTERNS

Before Independence, however, political parties were largely responsible for attracting Jewish immigrants and settling them into established communities. The party organization was an extension of a world-wide political movement. It was ideologically grounded and jealous of its position within the wider Zionist organization. The party was more than a vote-getting machine: it conducted immigration activities, provided housing and employment, ran its own collective settlements, industries, banks and social services, and promoted educational and cultural facilities.

In these circumstances, public policy making con-
sisted largely of public declarations of shared values
and programs agreed to by rival ideologies. There were
a variety of formal and informal mechanisms by which
such agreements were reached and implemented. Open
forums were provided by the press, the National Council
and the public activities of the World Zionist Organization, Histadrut, the Jewish Agency and the National
Council Executive. There were also public meetings,
party conventions and open meetings of interest groups.

Hard bargaining behind closed doors was usually
confined to the relatively small number of party leaders
and functionaries who staffed the public organs of the
Jewish community. Similarly, party disputes were settled
in private, either through direct personal confrontation
or through group meetings held informally in somebody's
home or office. The resulting public pronouncements were
highly ideological, but low in rationality. They were
declarations of intent or awkward compromises designed
to maintain coalitions. The private dealings, on the
other hand, concentrated on short-run feasibilities.
They relied on intuition and improvisation rather than
on mistrusted expert advice.

EFFECTS OF INDEPENDENCE

With the creation of the State of Israel, the nature
of public policy making was transformed. The state
itself was a sovereign entity; it was free to accept or
reject decisions made by foreign bodies concerning the
internal and foreign affairs of the country. This
applied as much to the United Nations and foreign governments as it did to the World Zionist Organization and
private donors. All other internal institutions, such as
political parties, Histadrut, the Jewish Agency, collectives and the armed forces, were subordinate to the
government. Public policy making was thereby concentrated on the state and its organs.

At the same time, politics was professionalized.
Party leaders could concentrate full time on politics,

for as Ministers, Members of the Knesset (Representative Assembly or Parliament), department heads and local government officials they could be compensated from public funds. Between them and the people, and to a lesser extent between them and the party, was imposed the whole machinery of government. These years saw the reorganization of the Israel Defense Force, the creation of a police force and the Israeli Civil Service, the multiplication of governmental bureaus and local governments, the extension of the legal system and the expansion of public and joint enterprises.

National institutions took on functions previously performed by political parties and handled the channeling of overseas funds. Thus any person or institution needing help--and in the formative years of the nation most did--had to have access to the political elite that controlled institutions. This was done through party position, e.g., *kibbutz* representatives on party councils, or membership in independent pressure groups, e.g., the legal profession. Public policy making became more complicated. Greater reliance had to be placed on formal mechanisms which reduced the pressure at the center, thus enabling the political elite to concentrate on immediate crises.

To some extent, the broad outlines of pre-Independence public policy making remained intact. A public pronouncement of ideological goals is registered in Israel's equivalent of the Declaration of Independence:

> The State of Israel will be open
> for Jewish immigration and for the
> Ingathering of the Exiles; it will
> foster the development of the coun-
> try for the benefit of all its in-
> habitants; it will be based on free-
> dom, justice and peace as envisaged
> by the prophets of Israel; it will
> ensure complete equality of social
> and political rights to all its in-
> habitants, irrespective of religion,
> race or sex; it will guarantee

freedom of religion, conscience,
education and culture; it will
safeguard the Holy Places of all
religions; and it will be faithful
to the principles of the Charter
of the United Nations.

These goals have since been further elaborated by
governmental declarations of policy, detailed coalition
agreements, preambles to Basic Laws and other new legislation and the Covenant between the Government of Israel
and the Zionist Executive. The fullest enumeration of
state policies is contained in the Basic Principles of
Government Program, as approved by the Knesset on 17
December 1959. This covered collective responsibility,
Zionist objectives, economic policy, immigration and
absorption, foreign policy, social services, education
and culture, religion, public morality, constitutional
and administrative issues and the minorities. These
public statements record the measure of consensus among
all political parties or the major components of governmental coalitions. They reiterate national ideology and
have both symbolic significance and educational value.
They are declarations of intent and reaffirmations of
long-term objectives.

The public forums are even more active now than
before Independence. The press is as popular as ever,
and has been joined by government broadcasting and tele-
vision services. The latter reach the illiterates, even
if they are somewhat tame in comparison with the more
sophisticated media. The press now includes political
scandal sheets devoted to exposing shortcomings in the
establishment. Attempts to suppress unfavorable news or
extremist opinions have only partially succeeded and they
have often boomeranged on the authorities.

The most popular forums are still public meetings
addressed by political rivals and open to questions from
the floor. Party conventions and pressure group con-
gresses receive their due publicity. While methods are
still being developed for the accurate recording of
public opinion, there can be no doubt that whoever wants

a say will be heard. The question is whether public
expressions of opinion have much influence on public
policy making.

    In Israel's formative years, the political elite
was more inclined to tell the public what was good for
them. During the current process of normalization, as
it is called in Israel, there has been a reaction against
the utopian outlook of the Second Aliyah generation and
their progeny. Although they dominated pre-Independence
public policy-making councils, and continue to occupy
high political office, their numbers have diminished.
The more dogmatic among them are a vanishing breed.

    The utopians and dogmatists are being replaced by
pragmatists. The new elite is flexible in outlook, more
individualistically inclined, less disciplined, i.e.,
more inclined to depart from party lines, and more susceptible to extra-party political pressures from interest
groups and minorities. No party can afford to ignore
shifts in public opinion, however slight, or to neglect
persistent demands for specific action. Consequently,
the party functionaries have assumed a more positive
role: they now convey public opinion to the leadership,
rather than hectoring the converted and persuading the
uncommitted. The airing of diverse popular views is
probably the Knesset's most valuable function today.
It serves as a sounding board and public educator.

POLITICAL ELITES

    Public policy making is still largely conducted by
the political elite, which is composed of major party
leaders and top national administrators. They are
assisted by less partisan experts who staff national
institutions or represent specific pressure groups outside the party structures. Although representative of
Israel's entire political spectrum, the majority of the
elite is drawn from Mapai, the largest political party,
and from its closest coalition partners. These groups
have been entrenched in the national institutions since
the 1930's.

An alternative government, composed of left- and right-wing parties would be out of the question. The possibility that another party might replace Mapai as coalition head is reduced by the prestige the party has accumulated as the establishment during Israel's years of growth; the patronage it is able to exercise in national institutions; the political, financial and social power it exercises; and its control over public services and information.

As leader of the government, Mapai has had to act both responsibly and responsively. To show their independence, its opponents have had to exaggerate their differences, and they have acted irresponsibly in order to attract attention. Mapai, for its part, has been able to act opportunistically: it shifts alliances according to changes in public opinion; it readjusts its policies as internal factions and leaders wax and wane in influence. As the entrenched government party, Mapai has also been able to attract apolitical social climbers and to enlist the aid of technical experts, whatever their political persuasion. On the other hand, Mapai has suffered most from internal party feuds and splits and must take the blame for national tragedies.

COALITION MAINTENANCE

The establishment has been concerned with coalition maintenance and partisan mutual adjustment. It has accepted policies to which it is ideologically opposed. It has also retained control of the most important power centers or has ensured that independent power centers have been led by sympathizers. It has arranged the distribution of functions between power centers so that areas conceded to rivals cannot operate effectively without the sanction of areas it controls. Mapai has been able to switch policies when it reshuffles the coalition or forces a party showdown.

In matters deemed secondary, or on which it has no declared aims, Mapai is content to let rivals and coalition parties make decisions. When it has not been able to achieve a majority on important issues, it has had to shelve them, make important concessions or agree to impracticable and unworkable compromises. Political bargaining of this kind does not promote any higher rationality content now than did pre-Independence public policy making. There is still a premium on intuition, political sensitivity and political feasibility. Nor has political bargaining promoted a greater degree of openness. Mapai and its coalition partners are reluctant to reveal new divisions, feuds and splits; no bargainer is free to show his whole hand until the bargain has been concluded. Secrecy is further enforced by security demands.

Politicization of national institutions is an unavoidable concomitant of coalition maintenance. The pre-Independence "key system," which has survived in a few places, was a similar acknowledgment of the political facts of life. As indicated earlier, under the key system, offices were distributed in accordance with the number of votes polled by the parties at the previous general election. While advantages the politicization gives to the establishment are obvious, rivals and coalition partners also gain from their direct and equal participation in policy-making processes. The more they are brought into the system, the more responsible they become. Society benefits, because fewer groups are alienated or isolated from the majority; more gain a stake in the system; more become willing to defend it in principle from external critics.

Even more important, the participants are able to influence and guide the implementation of policies directly, particularly in those areas that concern them most. Participants have built-in information networks and strategically placed decisionmakers. Their political leverage ensures that the application of public policy is more attuned to the wishes of the community than might be the case if one party or group ruled by itself.

There has never, in any event, been a tradition of
depoliticization. It is quite alien to the Jewish community in Israel, and it has an unfortunate psychologica
connection with the British. Their "neutrality" was
viewed as indifference to social ills and complaisance
over social action programs; their "experts" were insen-
sitive to values or else downright incompetent. The
British could not have been Zionist pioneers. Israel,
according to local belief, requires leaders with a mission, a cause, fire in the belly. And men like that
are politicians, so goes local belief.

PROBLEMS OF POLITICIZATION

Politicization does not ensure that office holders,
however politically sensitive, can transcend opportunism
and the party line; that they can manage large-scale
technical and bureaucratic services; or that they can
devise new policies or evaluate old ones. Politicians c
carry out bad as well as good policies. They can staff
important public services with party followers who are
politically astute, but technically illiterate. They ca
waste precious resources on illogical flights of fancy.
They can so outsmart themselves in the game of politics
that nothing is achieved.

Israel has suffered in all these ways from politicization. As the errors have come to light, the demand
for rationalization, objectivity, independent evaluation
and scientism has grown. The performance of politicized
and depoliticized activities has been compared, and the
former has been found wanting. The most serious overall
deficiency has been the lack of middle-range policies
occupying the ground between short-run improvisation and
long-term ideological objectives. The construction of
middle-range policies requires skills different from
those common among Israeli leaders.

The younger generation of leaders has realized this
shortcoming and has begun to remedy the deficiency. They
have gone beyond the lip service which the older

generation paid to the problem. In the past decade, there has been an upsurge of interest in the behavioral, social and management sciences. Information and research have been restructured to facilitate incorporation into public policy making. Several continuing experiments in institution building related to policy analysis, have included planning, PPBS (Planning, Programming, Budgeting Systems), research institutes and consultative and advisory committees. More recently, there have been proposals for a policy analysis institute.

FORCES FOR RATIONALITY

The movement toward greater rationality in public policy making is aided by a number of self-reinforcing background factors. The political elite includes fewer old-time political bosses and more politically shrewd organization men. Political lines are less rigid and the political map is undergoing a radical overhaul as a result of the Six Day War. Foreign donors are no longer content to give money without strings attached, or at least without some definite evidence that the money is needed and will be put to good use. Israeli leaders are aware that they need to improve links with Diaspora Jewry; they know they must take advantage of foreign know-how in the development of advanced technological industries. They realize that old patterns may have outlived their usefulness, and that now may be the time to look for something new. More and better trained administrators are available. And the Israel Defense Forces have shown the relevance of the most modern management techniques.

For too long, Israeli society has been tolerant of its outdated administrative heritage. It must be as tough on its leaders as it is on its military trainees. The old style of public policy making, however, is so entrenched, so habitual, and its proponents would add, so successful, that new methods are endlessly questioned, pondered, criticized and debated before they are grudgingly accepted and introduced. In the process, however, methods are improved and the transition eased.

The old leaders, whose faces and names are known to all, continue to take political responsibility. They give political legitimacy to the new ways; they absorb the publicity while the new men experiment, create, innovate, learn political sensitivity and gain experience. Unknown outside their immediate circle, the new men can concentrate their full energies on the job at hand. They are learning to combine technical proficiency with political astuteness and are getting ready to take over the leadership of a rapidly maturing state. Before long, they will replace the old guard. In some areas they already have done so; in others, the old guard is resisting, and the transition may not be peaceful. But it is a clash between attitudes, not generations.

CHAPTER VI

Approaches to Planning

Fundamentally, there are two approaches to planning. One is a macroapproach, which conceives of wholes, targets, problems and the manipulation of institutions and activities to attain preconceived projections. The other is a microapproach, which concentrates on units, programs, activities in progress, self-initiative and the coordination of diverse, overlapping and contradictory projects based on feasible use of resources and accepted social objectives. The former envisages a comprehensive national bureaucratic planning system, replete with statistical services, projections, models, control mechanisms, penalties and incentives. The latter relies on the dependability and trustworthiness of actors in knowing what they want and how to go about their tasks. It postulates a process of mutual competition wherein the good will eclipse the bad, and an overall policy allocation unit will be responsible for maintaining conditions conducive to the execution of projects. The macroapproach is elitist and autocratic, while the microapproach is non-bureaucratic, decentralized and amenable to quickly changing values and social conditions.

Under Israeli conditions of constant crisis and change, decentralized facet planning and partisan mutual

adjustment are preferred. It should not be surprising
that in their review of Israeli planning, Akzin and Dror
conclude that "there is very little integrative and comprehensive national planning."[1] There is indeed no central planning authority staffed with professional planners charged with comprehensive, integrative, national
planning. There are no national five-year plans detail-
ing major social objectives and defining specific tasks,
targets and deadlines for operating agencies. Yet there
is planning of this kind where it is most needed. And
there is considerable microplanning in most social activities. These plans may not be publicized, detailed, coordinated or integrated into one scheme, but they do
exist. Things do not happen by chance in Israel; too
much is at stake if an important part fails to perform
properly. The rejection of central macroplanning is well
grounded.

THE NEED FOR NATIONAL PLANNING

Planned national development is an acknowledged need
in a small country whose population is concentrated along
a narrow strip of fertile coastal plain, with tongues of
settlement penetrating into denuded mountains and desert
waste. This unpromising country is expected to receive
all Jews who wish to settle in the homeland and to provide all residents with a standard of living comparable
to the best. Obviously there is a need to husband
available resources, to restore the original fertility of
the land, to develop unexploited natural resources and to
discover new potentialities. National planning of some
kind is essential. Pressures to this end are exerted by
international aid, by internal political disputes, and by
the intense competition for use of available resources.

---

[1]Benjamin Akzin and Yehezkal Dror, *Israel: High Pressure Planning* (Syracuse, New York: Syracuse University
Press, 1966), p. 77.

As Akzin and Dror report, national planning has been most successful in national defense, agricultural production, water distribution, capital import and economic policy. It has played a lesser role in land utilization, population distribution, migrant absorption, postal and telecommunication services, education and man-power training, transportation and industry. Most of these areas have been the concern of a specific governmental bureaucracy, and coordination has been achieved at the top political level. Even so, considerable difficulty has been encountered for three reasons. First, the association of national planning with regimentation has reduced cooperation from liberals and antistatists. Second, the idea that national planning sets limits on goals has offended the pioneer, promotive, creative, optimistic self-assurance of the Zionist elite. Finally, the success of innovative pragmatic facet planning has confirmed the existing political preference for non-bureaucratic inspirational planning and localized problem-solving strategies.

PRAGMATIC FACET PLANNING

Bureaucratic planning assumes a framework of broad consensus on aims and means. This does not exist in Israel, where coalition governments have difficulty in obtaining nationwide support for any course of action. The spectrum of opinion is so wide that a clear stand on any issue threatens the stability, coherence and existence of the state itself. As the majority cannot impose itself on the minority without endangering the state, strong dissent is accommodated. The decentralization of facet planning permits broad objectives that enjoy a high degree of consensus to be translated into practical working programs, and it permits powerful dissent groups to influence the outcome. Political bargainers, not professional planners, carry out the planning: they work out the concessions, incremental changes, compensations and reciprocities represented by the final outcome.

Bureaucratic planning works best in stable conditions, where the unexpected is minimal. Israel, by contrast, moves from crisis to crisis. Anything can--and usually does--happen. The flow of immigrants is determined by the persecution of Jews elsewhere; capital imports are subject to outside pressures. Defense operations are largely determined by the actions of neighboring states and terrorist groups.

In crisis situations, the immediate need takes priority over practically everything else, including thinking ahead. The tendency grows if resources are sparse and fully committed. Getting through the next week or next three months is enough, and a few spectacular decisions are decisive. No one can afford to be tied down by longer term commitments: to persist with detailed plans with set targets and deadlines is folly that may hasten collapse. On-the-spot improvisation is more suitable than the delays attendant on national bureaucratic planning.

In addition, Israel lacks planning experts and administrators trained in macroplanning techniques. On the other hand, there is a highly competent Central Bureau of Statistics, and many people are experienced in facet planning. Further, Israel, for its size and capacity, is one of the leaders in the computer field. These planning mechanisms are concentrated where they promise the best returns in terms of problem manageability, opportunity costs, effective implementation, self-control and ongoing activities.

Another hindrance to macroplanning lies in the way planning directives are received. Israel lost confidence in overseas planning experts when their advice proved to be impractical, inferior to local thinking or unaware of political nuances. The same criteria are applied to local planners. In addition, except in highly confidential areas, widespread publicity accompanies internal controversies. Since contending parties invariably seek allies in the mass media and among their clientele, it is not easy to steamroll the opposition.

Evaluation of planning is as inadequate as it is
elsewhere. Exceptional as Israel's circumstances may be,
there is little attempt to seek comparability with Singapore or Hong Kong, whose experiences are not dissimilar.
Yet pragmatic facet planning, as Bertram M. Gross points
out, is the enemy of dogma, ideology and doctrine.[2] It
is multidisciplinary and incorporates scientific knowledge and high quality information. It sticks to reality
and benefits from the self-evaluation forced by continuous interaction between rivals.

Pragmatic facet planning meets needs and encourages
creativity. It relieves pressure on an already overbur-
dened central government. Adjustments are made in anticipation of others' reactions and it can be assumed that
no serious problem is being neglected by the interests
involved. If self-interest does not work in the best
interests of all, rivals can be relied on to expose distortion. No one need calculate the implications of the
whole, only of that part which concerns himself. If some
values need to be stressed more than others, the responsibility is placed where it ought to be--not on bureaucratic planners, but on responsive politicians.

[2]"Prefatory Comment" in Akzin and Dror, above,
pp. xxiii-xxxii.

CHAPTER VII

Organization: Form and Function

The fragmented nature of national planning and the diversification of organizational forms produces a distinctive style of operation in Israeli crisis conditions. Administrators are forced to think on their feet, to adjust to difficulties as they arise. Problems cannot easily be pushed onto someone else, for they remain a continuing threat to personal security and safety. Their ramifications extend beyond institutional, functional or disciplinary boundaries. Nor, in crisis conditions, can problems be anticipated or headed off.

This eminently practical style tends to complicate the overall view of organization. Temporary solutions of individual problems may intensify other problems, or push them onto the future. Basic issues may be postponed while manageable non-essentials are dealt with first. The effect may be to create twice as much work as would have been required had more rational approaches been adopted from the beginning. There may be too many hasty and narrowly conceived actions, too much rushing at fences, and too little forecasting of possible events.

These dangers are clearly present in Israel, for many small organizations compete in the same area, fight

interminable jurisdictional battles, and repeat each
other's actions--including mistakes. They suffer from
excessive built-in obsolescence, make-work and slack. On
the other hand, this form of social organization avoids
vacuums in social action; permits a wider range of social
choice; and gives expression to creative energy, pioneering zeal and reluctance to accept artificial limitations.
And it is able to accommodate diverse strategies.

VARIETIES OF ORGANIZATION

As in all states, the machinery of government (including the legal system, police, Israel Defense Forces
and public and mixed enterprises), is most important or-
ganizationally. In Israel, government takes on an added
significance. The country has never been at peace. It
has had to maintain a large standing army and a sizable
armaments industry; peacetime activities have had to be
geared to instant war activities. Consequently, the
whole society is in some way part of the war machine, and
is bound to the government's war preparations. War and
peace systems are inseparable: all decisions outside the
state apparatus ultimately reflect war strategy.

The socialist orientation of the major governmental
party has favored communal, cooperative and public enterprise over private enterprise and voluntarism. Private
enterprise has been hidebound by governmental regulations
and controls, and has failed to generate the dynamism expected from it. The government has stepped in to resus-
citate and revive flagging initiative. More importantly,
the government largely controls the flow of external
funds and determines the allocation and distribution of
resources.

There is no group or activity that does not depend
on government support of some sort, be it license, protection, subsidy, land grant, public utilities or law.
The government with its various offshoots is the largest
employer, the largest landowner, the largest investor and
the largest consumer. The citizen is confronted with the

public bureaucracy at every turn. This is true even though the government is reluctant to rationalize the quasi-governmental functions being performed by the Jewish Agency (immigration), Histadrut (public transportation, medical-health services, construction, marketing), political parties and voluntary organizations. Even willingness to divest itself of profitable commercial activities has not lessened the public bureaucracy's ubiquity.

It is impossible to draw any clear demarcation lines between public and private sectors. The governmental subsystem is fairly well distinguished by structure, finance, law and political control, but other factors blur the lines of demarcation. The Israeli government contracts out specific functions while retaining controlling influence and final responsibility; it delegates functions informally without maintaining controls; it cooperates with other bodies in joint ventures and mixed enterprises; subsidizes other bodies to ensure their continuance, such subsidization being accompanied by gifts, favorable loans, staff transfers and practical monopolies; and, finally, it uses other bodies as front organizations. Some private and semipublic bodies are kept in existence only because the government does not wish to perform their activities directly.

There are also many multipurpose organizations that perform social functions. Political parties are not mere vote-gathering machines: they are political movements that may operate collective settlements, trade unions, health schemes, banks, housing estates, industrial enterprises and youth movements. Trade unions are not mere employee protection organizations, but also provide social services and run a wide range of semipublic enterprises. They are major developmental entrepreneurs and marketing organizers responsible for 20 percent of the economy. The collectives are not simply agricultural colonies, but also serve as border posts, military units, manufacturers and ideologues. The Israel Defense Forces provide non-military services such as vocational courses, adult education, social integration and cultural absorption. They run labor units for national projects and

collectives and subsidize retail outlets. Religious organizations run schools, hospitals, welfare services,
workshops, charities and cultural facilities such as
libraries, bookshops and newspapers.

DISTRIBUTION OF FUNCTIONS

Functions are divided among many different bodies
whose interests overlap. Even within the governmental
subsystem there is no clear, let alone rational, distribution of functions among central ministries. Economic
policy is divided among nine ministries; social services,
four; scientific research, four; minority group matters,
three. Even security is divided between two ministries--
the result of historical accident, political bargaining
between coalition partners, bureaucratic empire-building,
ministerial preference and intentional undermining of a
rival ministry. In practice, disputes over conflicting
jurisdiction are settled by the superiority of one ministry, by agreements between middlemen, and by compromises
between rivals.

The citizen has to run from office to office, trying
to track down first the right ministry and then an official willing to make a decision or accept the responsibility for advice previously given. Often the citizen
cannot transact his business on the spot but must travel
to and fro, from one office to another, only to find that
some of the journeying was unnecessary, or that all of it
must be repeated because of a mistake at the beginning.
Outside the governmental sector, the situation is not as
frustrating, but the same problems occur. Newcomers are
particularly discouraged by the red tape until they learn
to overcome the snarls by going straight to the top and
getting instant action via *protekzia*.

PROTEKZIA

The formal front presented by the organization is
one of bureaucratism. If the client is unknown to the
organization, he must fill out forms and queue up to

receive attention. The process may be repeated every
time he appears. Once the organization knows the client
he can substitute letters and telephone calls for personal confrontations. Those who lack time and patience
may be able to by-pass the ritual and cut through the
formality by using intermediaries known to the organization or through personal contacts within the organizatio

This is *protekzia*, the use of informal contacts
to by-pass the normal procedures, which are usually
slow, unfriendly and autocratic. For those who can
employ *protekzia*, life runs smoother: informal contact
saves time and exasperation, avoids queuing, ensures a
fair hearing and may possibly be advantageous in the
distribution of scarce resources. *Protekzia* is somethin
personal, related largely but not solely to range of con
tacts, length of residence in Israel, proximity to power
elites, status, and possible reciprocity in favors ren-
dered.

Protekzia was one of many safety devices adopted by
the Jewish communities in Palestine to conduct illegal
activities. It was similar to the conduct of ghetto
affairs and to the ghetto's relationship with autocratic
officialdom. Written statements were avoided; business
was conducted on a personal basis, each side trusting
the other to respect the rules of the game and follow
mutual agreements. Decisions were confined to ingroups
although leakages might occur along the grapevine. Bargaining took place outside bureaucratic mechanisms, whic
were too cumbersome to respond to opportunities under
quickly changing circumstances. These informal ways of
working have been retained by many members of Israel's
bureaucratic elites.

As a result, important decisions are made outside
formal channels and conveyed by word of mouth to ingroups. This process consolidates the power of the ingroup, prevents revelation of deep internal divisions
and highlights self-control through mutual anticipation
of the reactions of participants, each of whom accepts
the rules of the game and acts as spokesman for particular interests. In this way, coordination is achieved

even if one interest threatens to distort agreed patterns, and the ingroups (in this case the interlocking elites of Israel's public leadership), are able to deal quickly with change and crisis. In some respects it closely resembles the organizational forms that Bennis believes will gradually replace bureaucracy: "adaptive, temporary systems of diverse specialists, solving problems, linked together by coordinating and task-evaluative specialists, in organic flux."[1] On the other hand, it supplements a bureaucratic society and is somewhat less temporary than many people excluded from the ingroup would prefer.

EFFICIENCY

As might be expected, the employment of scientific management within organizations varies according to function, size, centrality, size of clientele and ethnic origins of founders, owners and top level management. Bureaucratic organizations are more prone to use scientific management than are other forms of social organization, particularly those with international connections and strong association with the governmental subsystem. Large-scale organizations have systematized and standardized themselves more than small organizations, but there are exceptions where owners have preferred more personal arrangements; where employee-owners strive to retain control over their employed managers; or where politicization is strong. Persons coming from organizational societies or *sabras* educated overseas tend to be more sympathetic to scientific management. High priority organizations receive favored treatment. The best in Israel compare with the best anywhere, while low priority organizations rank far down the scale. Organizations handling large numbers of people are required to function better although they receive more adverse publicity and face more trouble in satisfying both clientele and staff.

---

[1] Warren G. Bennis, *Changing Organizations* (New York: McGraw-Hill, 1966), p. 12.

Other factors to be considered include the degree o competitiveness, trade protection, governmental support, clientele expectations, restrictive labor and trade prac tices and politicization. These determine how much inef ficiency is tolerated. Outside priority areas, it tends to be high: people do not expect better; cannot envisage anything better; do not really care; have grown accustomed to bad performance; or have adapted themselves to poor performance. People recognize the difficulties in the environment, the problems faced by an organization with sparse resources, deficiencies in staffing, poor leadership, outdated rules, political intrigue, multiracialism and the rest. In some areas, people do not want maximum efficiency; they place other values above good performance, or they fear efficient enforcement of laws.

The trend appears to be toward less tolerance for inefficiency. It is recognized that meaningful independence requires an efficient base and that the scandals, injustices and wastes of protectionism are self-destructive. Such evils undermine the morale of those who do not benefit, but have to foot the bill as taxpayers, customers, servicemen, patients and parents.

ISRAEL DEFENSE FORCES AND THE HISTADRUT

To illustrate the differences in approach, the Israel Defense Forces should be compared with the Histadrut empire. One of the first actions of the new govern ment after the 1949 Armistice was the depoliticization o: the armed forces.[2] The I.D.F. consists of a professiona. corps, conscripted youth and various grades of reserves including virtually all adult citizens below retirement age.

-----

[2]Amos Perlmutter, *Military and Politics in Israel: Nation-Building and Role Expansion* (New York: Frederick A. Praeger, 1969), gives the most complete account in English of the organization, leadership and role of the I.D.F.

Since military service looms so large in Israeli adult life, the I.D.F. has an important influence on the administrative culture. It provides Israelis with a familiar standard of reference by which other organizations can be judged. It presents new opportunities for civilians to show what they can do, irrespective of their backgrounds and civilian employment. It is a favored institution, with political backing, priority in resources, staff loyalty, military discipline and other exceptional attributes.

So far its performance has been praiseworthy: with its split-second timing, high effectiveness, and speedy mobilization it is one of Israel's finest achievements. It relies heavily on the latest developments in military science plus a few innovations of its own. The I.D.F. is probably Israel's leading proponent of scientific management, and it insists on staff rotation with ready replacement by understudies. Retiring military staff are eagerly sought for diverse administrative posts in the hope that they can inject military success into civilian organizations. But because non-military circumstances are so different, they are not always successful.

In addition, the influence is not all one way. The I.D.F. has had to adjust to its large civilian contingents; it must conduct its affairs differently than if all recruits were professional military men. Its administration is peculiar to itself, and, needless to say, it is classified information.

The Histadrut, the General Federation of Israeli Labor, is the second largest civilian employer in Israel, responsible for over 20 percent of the economy. In recent years, it has been one of the primary seekers of military administrative talent to boost its poor performance and to provide successors to the old guard. Unlike the I.D.F., it has always been politicized; unlike the Israeli Civil Service, it has made no serious progress toward depoliticization. It is staffed on a modified key system. Partisanship is strong; political and ideological values predominate. Of all pre-Independence

institutions, the Histadrut has done the most to preserve
the old administrative culture; and because of its position as prominant employer, trade union federation and
copartner in development, it has effectively prevented
any sharp change.

Egalitarianism remains its credo and is incorporated
into the wage and taxation structure of the country.
Informality and ingroup decisionmaking have been habitual: only relatively recently has Histadrut agreed to
publish an annual report and balance sheet of its activities. The old guard has been sufficiently entrenched to
ignore much public and member dissatisfaction and to
brush aside the external investigations that revealed administrative chaos in many areas. Because the Histadrut
has neither submitted to public inspection nor scientif-
ically evaluated its activities, it is not possible to
gauge the validity of the underground smear campaign
which its leadership attributes to political opponents.
In the opinion poll conducted among undergraduate students, its administrative performance was considered poor
even by those who viewed it sympathetically as an institution. Similar views have also been expressed within
the Histadrut. Long overdue introspection will no doubt
take place soon.

FACTORS INFLUENCING PERFORMANCE

Uneven organizational performance cannot be attributed simply to differences between generations, or to
different approaches to scientific management. Age and
training alone are only two of a large number of vari-
ables that determine results. Nevertheless, an injection
of scientific management into Israel's administrative
culture would be desirable. Improvisation and creativity
need to be harnessed to a more stable and rational administrative framework; otherwise, their usefulness may be
dissipated by disorganization; much good planning may be
wasted by bad execution and inadequate consolidation.

There can be no doubt that there is incessant activity in the Israeli administrative culture. Administrators work for years, tirelessly, without breaks, and under immense pressure. Some claim that work cannot be delegated to subordinates because of their inadequate training and aptitude. Rarely does anyone admit that part of the burden may be self-manufactured; that work is deliberately created to keep people employed or to give the appearance of indispensability; that overlapping and duplication are responsible for needless repetition; that if the administrators modified their self-image of the chosen few leading the many to the promised land, they might be able to delegate more and train subordinates to assume greater responsibilities.

A dose of rationality is needed to reduce overblown organizations whose tasks are not commensurate with their personnel; to induce amalgamation among splinter organizations; to simplify procedures for clientele; to overhaul the machinery of government; to block legal and procedural loopholes that invite corruption; and to close the gap in performance between good and bad organizations. But this would require a strong government, prepared to do battle with vested interests within and without. It would also require a crisis-free breathing space when the necessary reorganization could take place; larger numbers of administrative technicians and experienced administrative reformers willing to supervise the transformation; and more public support of effective performance. In the meantime, the administrative culture seems to be coping well enough, particularly in those areas where scientific management gives no guidance and where novel problems require novel solutions. In these respects, Israel's pragmatic administrative politicians may be one step ahead of the administrative theorists.

CHAPTER VIII

Intricacies of Budgeting

THE CONTEXT

Israeli budgeting takes place in a country living well beyond its means, constantly searching for ways to meet commitments with meager resources, and incurring debts for future redemption. The gap between goals and resources is filled by substantial capital imports, long-term debt financing, inflation and devaluation. Much attention is devoted to raising money from abroad. At home, taxation is high. The government promotes economic activity through monetary and fiscal policies, concessions to overseas investors, and subsidies to domestic producers. It combats tax evasion, illegal financing, corrupt business practices and unsound investment schemes.

For the organization, budgeting means getting money wherever one can, on whatever terms can be obtained. It means keeping the budget confidential, if only to prevent further expenditure claims; distributing the money between equally important demands; and ensuring that funds are spent on earmarked purposes. Budgeting in Israel is only for experts with daring, self-confidence and strong nerves. Anything goes.

Those with knowledge of ghetto financing would be at home in Israel. Much the same circumstances apply: there is not enough to go round; the same resources must go from hand to hand; and nobody can afford to break the chain. One person borrows from another, creating one chain of credit that in turn creates other chains. Everybody manages to survive by acting first and worrying about the wherewithal later. In the end, nobody goes short of necessities. Somewhere in the system compassion tempers strict legality and ownership. Manipulation of papers is involved, as is some fiddling with the books. Indeed, some of the smartest manipulators end by outsmarting themselves, and the whole edifice collapses dramatically. Banks, shipping companies and public enterprises have fallen; many other organizations might have done so, if their allies had not come to the rescue in time.

The government is partly responsible for this state of affairs. Like other governments, it disguises the amount and direction of defense costs and other secret funds. Its elaborate regulations and tax codes, designed to curb bad business practices, create an incentive for outsmarting the authorities. The legal and accounting professions strive to maintain high standards and to uphold their reputation, but societal pressures cannot always be resisted.

PUBLIC FINANCE

Public finance is no exception. There is no comprehensive legislation covering governmental budgeting. Except for the budget, the Knesset (Parliament) has no control over substantial governmental monies. The budget itself leaves much to be desired in terms of estimating procedures, forecasting and planning, information, progress reports, loan provisions and unauthorized funding. Legally, few sanctions are imposed for disregarding budget law, and there is low personal liability for financial irresponsibility.

The Annual Reports of the State Comptroller catalog some of the tricks played by top level financial officials. For example, government bodies have raised money by requiring suppliers to provide surplus credit in order to win contracts. The Department of Finance bought and stored unextracted natural gas from a public oil prospecting corporation. Thus it could aid the corporation even though it had no authorization for a subsidy. It also granted money to a government-controlled bank by buying shares at 180 percent instead of the 110 percent market price. The department has guaranteed loans obtained by public bodies from private banks at excessive interest rates; later, it has had to meet defaulted payments.

To balance the record, it should be noted that Israeli administrators were early experimenters with performance budgets and with such budgetary incentives as crediting savings to the following year. The Bureau of the Budget has been particularly innovative. Indeed, its formal budget presentation has turned full circle from departmental accounts to tripartite division into defense, development and normal activities, and then back again into amalgamated accounts based on departmental programs. The overall quality of departmental budgeting has vastly improved, though it is still uneven. There are no rewards for good budgets and few sanctions against bad ones. Mistakes, after all, favor hard-pressed ministries.

CONTROL BY PUBLIC WATCHDOGS

Israeli administrators do not get away with their antics scot-free. Constantly peering over their shoulders are public watchdogs, the most specialized of which are the Comptrollers. These have full powers of access and inquiry in their respective spheres, and are obligated to make their findings public. They are the supreme auditors, legal detectives, management evaluators and public guardians. Their reports receive wide publicity, especially when they reveal scandal and gross incompetence. Their effectiveness varies, being dependent on the personality of the incumbent, the quality of his supporting staff, the partisan nature of the office, length of tenure and possibility of reappointment, work methods, and, above all, fearlessness in publication. Some Comptrollers, drawn into ingroup controversies, are forced to be discreet in their disclosures.

Of particular importance is the State Comptroller's Office, established in 1949 as a supreme audit body for the public sector. Independent of the executive and directly responsible to the Knesset, it was envisaged as a depoliticized fourth power with far-ranging authority to investigate the disbursement of public monies. The general criteria for inspections have been legality, regularity, moral integrity and efficiency and economy.

Standards for the latter have been laid down by the State Comptroller. For instance, in examining efficiency, a start is made with work organization and methods. This investigation then moves to the economic significance of operations and results, and perhaps to the standard of service offered to the public. The investigator determines whether the inspected body, in achieving its goal, has spent the minimum of funds; whether it has done its utmost to prevent squandering; and whether its capacity has been fully utilized. In practice, the scope of inspection has been limited by the Comptroller's operating principles of postaudit, and by a reluctance to allocate individual responsibility, issue orders, intervene in areas of administrative discretion, or interfere in professional matters.

The State Comptroller's large staff has built up a reputation of impartiality and fairness in its dealings with public agencies. It has been largely responsible for improved morality and administrative performance in the government subsystem. On the other hand, outsmarting the Comptrollers has added another dimension to administrative behavior. The Knesset has not dealt promptly with its findings and delays have sometimes nullified

its original recommendations. But the process is far
from futile. The very existence of the State Comptroller's Office is an important factor. Its examinations
are never treated with contempt; its findings are rarely
ignored. Its reputation for fairness is such that, along
with the judicial system and the Israel Defense Forces,
it is one of the few public institutions in which the
citizen has full and complete confidence.

CHAPTER IX

Staffing in Public and Semi-Public Posts

CRITICAL VIEWS

No society has entirely succeeded in substituting achievement for ascriptive criteria of status. Nepotism, patronage, chicanery, corruption and subjectivity have not been eliminated in bureaucracies. Where merit is assessed by educational qualification, limited access to higher education confines selection and excludes large numbers of capable people. Israel, like any other country, can be criticized on this score. Critics also point eagerly to the strong protective unions and the social mores that make dismissal difficult after one year's satisfactory employment and that give undue weight to seniority in promotion. Discrimination on the basis of sex, race, ethnic origin, religion and political affiliation exists despite laws and admonitions to the contrary. Vestiges of the key system still remain. Rarely can one find objective tests, efficiency ratings, work value assessments, pay research bureaus, career planning or other features associated with merit systems. However, this is not the full story. There is another side.

ACHIEVEMENT CRITERION

If Israel has an aristocracy, it is the members and offspring of the Second Aliyah of Jewish settlers. They have played an important part in national institution building and public policy making and have projected their values into a national ideology. They saw themselves as self-sacrificing colonizers, devoted to creating a new society in which the reward was to be neither status, wealth nor property, but simply the results of labor, be it agricultural, military, cultural or communal. They translated their ideal into institutional reality by creating collective farm settlements, cooperative enterprises, labor exchanges, mutual aid services, workers' organizations, defense units and representative national coordinating bodies.

More significantly, the criterion for internal recognition of status was achievement (results), not past origins or present wealth and connections. Achievement involved learning a new language, accepting a low, uncertain standard of living, adapting to a new culture, working hard and getting things done successfully.

Each succeeding wave of immigrants had to come to terms with the ideology and institutions of the Second Aliyah. Newcomers had to make their own independent contribution and compete for leadership on terms laid down by the Second Aliyah. In the past 20 years, the pioneering values have been much modified by bureaucratization, the influx of large numbers of non-Zionist newcomers, economic growth and the ability to capitalize on past achievements. Ascription may be growing stronger, due to increased emphasis on participation in pioneer colonization, active military service in major campaigns and other past rather than current achievements. But newcomers still have to prove themselves, to make their own way in a task-oriented society according to their personal talent, energy, intellect, organizing ability and creativity. Those who come with sufficient capital to maintain themselves are exceptions, but their lack of achievement in the accepted sense limits their participation in public life, certainly in public policy making.

Despite protective measures that safeguard the defenseless and the lowest social strata, penalties for failure are severe. Senior military officers may be stripped of their rank or dismissed on the field of battle; politicans and officials may be removed from office without warning and may have to struggle to clear themselves even if no charges are pressed. Businessmen may be bailed out, but at a price. Life at the top is tough, and the social repercussions of alleged failure are cruel. The shocks are cushioned for lesser men: the further down the social scale, the greater the protection that is accorded mediocrity, senility, incapacity and inertia. This does not mean that all members of the Israeli elite are outstanding, or that they are fully qualified for their jobs, merely that they have fought hard to get there and are still able to hold down their jobs.

EQUAL OPPORTUNITY

The demonstration of personal worth is fairly easy for Jews, much less so for non-Jews. Israeli elites are constantly searching for potential: able performers are quickly spotted in schools, youth movements, paramilitary and military units, party organizations, collectives and cooperatives, work places and voluntary societies. The able usually have many opportunities to show their worth. Young persons are entrusted with responsible tasks and tested under different conditions; the employee can participate in union, party or military unit as well as his job; the town dweller can join a collective settlement; while the frustrated *kibbutznik* can work in the movement's bureaucracy, in the party, or--if he is willing to move--in the town. Not everyone, however, is able to recognize or use his opportunities. Others lack them altogether.

The obviously disadvantaged are those who reject or are rejected by the prevailing cultural pattern. These include newcomers unable to assimilate or adapt to an alien culture and often handicapped by lack of language

facility, contacts, capital or knowledge; the Bedouin,
religious sects and other groups cut off from the bureaucratic society; non-Jews; and offspring of national
figures, who are judged harshly, lest the charge of
nepotism be leveled against their parents. In addition,
the disadvantaged include those who experience unequal
opportunity anywhere, namely incompetent employees and
persons dependent on social welfare and charity; school
dropouts and illiterate adults; and those subject to
social discrimination: non-professional women, elderly
people, the physically and mentally handicapped, and
foreigners.

Among the most disadvantaged are Jews from the Nort
African and Middle Eastern ghettos. Unable to adjust to
a modern bureaucratic state, they *feel* disadvantaged.
The Israeli government has taken special steps to meet
their grievances by paying particular attention to the
second generation and by accelerating the advancement
of the first generation in public and semipublic employment. In other respects, an end to discrimination requires a permanent settlement of the Palestinian question, full employment, expansion of the educational system, changes in social attitudes and similar long-term
developments. But even with the best will, it is impossible to eliminate the feeling of discrimination, whethe
or not it is based on fact.

POLITICAL ENTREPRENEURSHIP

Before independence, public offices in the Jewish
community were usually distributed according to the key
system. Thus every splinter group had a part in public
policy making, and each shared in the spoils of office.
After the establishment of the state, politicization was
lessened considerably. Larger numbers of apolitical
ex-Mandate officials were employed, as were newcomers
with tenuous political affiliations. Nonetheless, at
top levels ministries became party strongholds and local
governments veered towards the key system. Political
entrepreneurship ensured that the new state was served

by loyal and generally highly competent people, but it
also ensured that no able person who wanted public
employment was denied it.

The current situation has not appreciably altered.
No vacancy in the Israeli Civil Service is advertised
until it has been ascertained that there are no qualified candidates among officials currently employed. Va-
cancies remain unfilled because there are no suitable
applicants; qualified people, preferring other employment, reject approaches from public institutions, which
are continuously in search of good people. The expanding
professional career service is recruited through the
labor exchanges and the Civil Service Commission,
although some politicization still exists, with detrimental effects. It has debased the image of public employment, fragmented the public bureaucracy, prevented free
internal movement, hindered the evolution of a formalized
merit system, and aided protectionism and underemployment. On the other hand, politicization has been proven
a flexible instrument. It has instilled a strong sense
of mission in top officials, smoothed political-
administrative relationships and helped integrate the
underprivileged.

The extent of politicization in the private sector
is not known. The Histadrut, *kibbutz* movements and party
machines are highly politicized. One would suspect that
mass media organs, party enterprises, e.g., banks, and
defense industries are also highly politicized at the
top, but not necessarily at lower levels. Genuine private enterprise would presumably be less concerned with
party affiliations and political beliefs, but more susceptible to other prejudices.

Even so, the extent of politicization in both public
and semipublic sectors fuses politics and administration.
There is interchange in both directions (though it is
less usual for a politician to return to administration),
and multiple officeholding is still accepted. There are
no clearly defined career patterns or pathways leading
into the bureaucratic elites. Military bureaucrats may

switch to public bureaucracies, local government or private enterprise. Party bureaucrats may find themselves in public enterprises, trade union organizations or voluntary associations. Scarcity of administrative talent is so great that the person with accomplishments in one area is eagerly sought after and may undertake a variety of commissions.

The mixed nature of many enterprises calls for this very type of versatile administrative politician, able to find business and resources where he can, knowledgeable, capable of quick decisions, well connected with power elites and experienced in coalition tactics. He must be familiar with insecurity and conscious of competing pressures: accustomed, in short, to dealing with potentially explosive situations, intense political competition, strained working relations and unsatisfactory working conditions.

CHAPTER X

Administration and Reform

THE QUESTION OF CIVIL LIBERTIES

Israeli leaders know the meaning of persecution, arbitrariness in government, and deprivation of civil rights from firsthand experience in Czarist Russia, Nazi Germany, British Palestine and other countries. Zionism is grounded in the concept of national liberty. Freedom has long been a hallowed ideal among the Jewish people and Jews have been prominent in civil rights struggles. The Spanish Inquisition impressed on them the need for religious freedom; the ghetto, the need for social, economic and political rights; the Holocaust, the need for racial equality. For most Jewish immigrants, Israel represents freedom, a release from bondage, persecution and minority psychosis. There, as nowhere else, they are at home. Despite petty bureaucratism and interminable governmental regulations, they feel free. They would like to extend this new-found freedom to all minorities in Israel and to rid themselves of restrictions on travel and free speech. But first, genuine peace must come to the Middle East. As long as the possibility of war remains, civil liberties must be subject to controls.

The war threat is only one of several factors limit
ing freedom in Israel. Many British Mandate laws remain
in force, giving the Israeli government wide discretion
under emergency powers. The only curb on the misuse of
such power is the pressure of public opinion and possibl
political repercussions. Censorship of mass media and
military laws, in turn, can prevent misuse of power from
being known publicly.

Other threats to freedom can be found in the administrative culture. First, the self-perpetuating bureaucratic elites overlap and intertwine to such an extent
that Israeli leadership, irrespective of political affil
iations, could unite in self-protection. Second, the
state is so involved in communal affairs that the citize
cannot avoid its tentacles. He has no knowledge of
administrative law to aid him in his dealings with the
state. Finally the public bureaucracy suffers in many
areas from bureaupathology, hasty improvisation, party
feuds, the inexperience of administrators, and heavy reliance on self-protection and individual initiative.
Maladministration and abuse of bureaucratic power take
many forms. These range from slight errors through care
lessness or the strain of overwork, to grave deficiencies, prejudice and criminal intent. Yet none of these
things may attract attention. The relevant documents ma
be wrongly filed or mislaid. The officials concerned ma
not be aware that any error has been made, or, worse,
they may deliberately conceal their error. Being inexpe
rienced in the ways of democracy, the citizen may accept
unfair treatment, an adverse decision or a breach of his
civil liberties without question or protest. If he
senses something wrong, he may not know how to obtain
remedial action.

Concern for the preservation of civil liberties is
a marked feature of the administrative culture. Adminis
trators know well how easily abuses can arise; how diffi
cult it is to compensate wronged citizens. The politica
consequences of abuse are grave, and the reputation of
Israeli administration is not enhanced by accusations of
autocracy.

Although there is no Bill or Code of Rights, Israel
follows the practice of British common law, which rests
on an assumption of civil liberty. Several rights are
guaranteed by law; legal recourse is available against
their infringement. The legal profession has been a
mainstay in the battle for civil liberties, but its remedial powers are limited. The oppressed citizen must
seek more powerful (and less costly) allies. His party,
trade union and immigrant association can be relied on to
use their influence, standing, contacts and knowledge,
i.e., their *protekzia*, to achieve better results. When
these fail, the mass media can be relied upon to embar-
rass and harass recalcitrant administrators, although
only within the confines of political expediency.

Alternatively, citizens may complain to the organization at fault until they get action or a promise of
action. Or they may send their complaints to whoever
they believe can obtain action. The Prime Minister is
an obvious target, as is the State Comptroller. Both
offices have routinized their handling of complaints.
The Prime Minister's Office has established a complaints
section, while the State Comptroller's Office investi-
gated complaints as part of its overall responsibilities
until 1969, when the office was transformed into the Ombudsman. In addition, several other authorities and
organizations have set up complaints offices in order to
reduce abuse and remedy just complaints.

There is a genuine feeling that the underprivileged
are not getting a fair deal; that something must be done
to check the development of second- or third-class citi-
zenship. Otherwise, grievances will be expressed in a
violent form, and antigovernment attitudes will become
ingrained. The problem is particularly acute in border
regions and in the newly administered territories. Outside these areas, more lasting solutions may be found by
strengthening democratic institutions; neutralizing officials; raising the quality of administrative performance;
and improving adult education and the integration of newcomers. In addition, the harmful effects of *protekzia*
must be rooted out; the occupational prestige of administration enhanced and the machinery of government reshaped.

ATTITUDES TOWARD REFORM

No one attempts to hide the many shortcomings in Israel's administrative performance; they are all too obvious. To some extent, gross distortions are deliberate, for they provide comic relief from the stresses of everyday living in a crisis situation. They reveal the Jew's ability to laugh at himself, to refuse to take things so seriously that the joy goes out of life altogether.

The validity of complaints, however, depends on the individual's perspective. To the *vatiquim*, who recall persecution and the tribulations of settlement in the new land, the present is an immeasurable improvement, an unqualified success, and a major achievement. They respond to complaint and criticism by recalling the past and describing how much better things are now. To newcomers from well developed countries with long established administrative traditions, Israeli administration is anachronistic, bewildering and badly in need of drastic reforms. The *vatiquim* know how to work the system, and have the personal connections to get things done quickly and effectively. The newcomers have yet to learn how the system operates; they continue to project their foreign values and expect Israeli administrators to conform to them. The former is apathetic to the need for administrative reform; the latter is full of reform proposals.

With change widespread, how is the need for administrative reform to be recognized? It is necessary to note, first, that rigid structures and ancient rules are not in themselves bad. Even in turbulent times, they may provide the stability and continuity that prevent chaos. Second, performance cannot simply be compared with the aspiration levels represented by ideological goals, planning targets or statements of intent. Nor can it be evaluated by looking only at grievances and evidence of failure. Both sets of indices are, in fact, highly subjective. The first set may not even exist. Where it does, the fact that realistic plans and estimates have not been attained may be no reflection on administrative performance. The second set of criteria is just as unsatisfactory, for a people may have an unrealistic aspiration level, or be prone to complaining.

Among serious administrative problems still confronting Israel are these: (a) low rationality content in policy making; (b) the prevalence of too many small competitive units, unwilling to lose their identity in amalgamation; (c) low evaluation of administration; (d) lack of preparation of administrators; (e) disorganized financing; (f) inadequacy of safeguards against abuse of discretionary power; (g) inequality of access to bureaucratic elites; (h) bureaupathology; (i) neglect of evaluation; and (j) unevenness of performance. Other problems may be more fundamental and more urgent, but they too indicate that superficial or formal rearrangements or corrections will not improve matters unless the underlying causes are also tackled; that administrative reform is associated with other kinds of societal reform; and lasting reforms will take many years to accomplish.

Support for administrative reform is growing. It is becoming more difficult to shrug off complaints and explain away mistakes. People are more demanding: they no longer temper their strictures and demands with acknowledgment of the problems faced by administrators. And the more the leadership sticks to the same formulae, the same excuses and platitudes, the more they alienate the masses who have borne much in the past but now want change. Young people in particular are bored with stories of how bad things used to be; they want action. They have the support both of those disadvantaged by the present administrative culture, and of those who have unceasingly attempted to improve administrative performance.

Once they catch on, reform demands are infectious. The same is true of emulation of successful reforms. The difficulty lies in overcoming the primary inertia and devising practical reforms. Since the major parties have all been responsible for government policies, administrative criticism constitutes an attack on one's own political stewardship. Chauvinism and Zionism, backed by a defensive mechanism evolved in centuries of oppression and persecution, combine to keep criticism within the family circle. Constant harping on the same subject provokes instantaneous defensive reactions. Those in a position to lead reforms are too involved personally or too committed to the status quo to risk dramatic action. With so much else to be done, so much else demanding immediate attention, reform receives a low priority.

Before any meaningful reform movement can be launched, certain basic requirements must be met. Much more must be known about the internal workings of Israel. administration. The lack of information and research is linked to censorship and secrecy, official parochialism and political suspicion, fear of exposure and unclear public relations policies. Priorities in administrative reform must be established. Should, for instance, a start be made on the reorganization of the machinery of government (a task now in hand)? Or is it more important to undertake the further depoliticization of the Israeli Civil Service, or general institution building in the field of scientific management? Or should there be a deliberate government commitment to administrative reform? The ground needs to be prepared beforehand to ensure acceptance of reform. Capable administrative reformers must be developed; they do not appear spontaneously. All these requirements are still lacking, although prospects for fulfillment within the next decade appear bright providing Israel gains some breathing space.

CHAPTER XI

Administrative Innovation

Administratively, Israel cannot yet match the ability of more developed countries to transform resources into social objectives according to the tenets of orthodox scientific management--economy, productivity, efficiency and rationality. The reasons for this include the absence of a developed administrative tradition; the persistence of crisis; preference for ideology over rationality and improvisation over planning and politics over professionalism; multipurpose rival institutions; scarcity of capital and administrative experience; and a considerable level of individualism.

Under Israeli conditions, the value premises of scientific management--rationality, stability, order, bureaucratism, neutrality--are largely inapplicable. Far too few people are capable of following them. They would enthrone the technocrat in a society where technocracy is still suspect. They would further divide political rivals and alienate the political extremes. They would solidify bureaucracies beyond their capacity to deal with crisis and rapid change. Indeed, some grave defects in Israeli social performance can be attributed to bureaupathology in long entrenched bureaucracies. These include the dogmatism of the Histadrut, the ritualism of

the Jewish Agency, the rigidity of customs and postal
administration, the standardization of local government
and the petty-mindedness of uncaring bureaucrats.

In addition, technocratic values would seriously
handicap any rapprochement between the "two nations," ar
they would virtually exclude non-Westernized newcomers
from public office. They would distort the educational
system and the pattern of employment. A more autocratic
political style might be needed to deal with discontente
groups. The security of the state might be jeopardized,
and willingness to meet external threats undermined.

If Israel's administrative culture is judged by its
efficacy in enabling the society to attain its goals, it
has performed more creditably, and has probably exceeded
external expectations. It would be tedious to elaborate
this point, involving as it would a brief history of the
entire first generation of the state of Israel. Much ha
been accomplished, though much more could undoubtedly
have been accomplished, with the benefit of hindsight.
By this measure, Israel's administrative performance is
at least as good as that of any other newly independent
state, probably better than that of many more developed
countries.

A more important measurement is whether Israel has,
during its formative years, evolved an administrative
culture that enables it to accelerate its development
capacity. It may have achieved spectacular successes at
the cost of future benefits; it may have lived off accumulated capital or depended on external support of a
temporary nature. Its future prospects, belying present
successes, may be dim.

CRISIS ADMINISTRATION

To date, Israel has evolved a crisis administration.
This may be its unique contribution to administrative
science. Crisis administration entails a pattern of administrative behavior that is highly conducive to

accelerated development. Israel does not even profess to attempt to tackle all problems. It concentrates on high priority problems, such as security, and on problems that brook no delay, such as arms embargoes. Unless outside bodies fill the gap, other problems are temporarily subordinated. The government tries to avoid creating unnecessary problems for itself: it refuses, for instance, to enforce bureaucratization.

In the meantime, administrators in areas of lesser priority are encouraged to use initiative to solve their own problems. Planning is undertaken only where it has been proven indispensable; it is not undertaken for its own sake. Outside the polity, permanent national bodies charged with anticipating problems and allocating resources for their solution are not needed. In the small compact state, with well developed communications and easy access to decisionmakers, problems are readily identified. The grapevine cuts through political rivalries and bureaucratism; felt grievances can easily be aired publicly. *Protekzia*, too, opens doors and enables clients to gain immediate action. Partisan mutual adjustment relieves top decisionmakers of much detail and routine, enabling them to concentrate on key issues and points of leverage.

In addition, many multipurpose and mixed organizations make important contributions. They integrate society by preventing alienation and maximizing participation; ensure clientele choice; accommodate growing differentiation; stabilize insecure institutional frameworks; reconcile political factions; reduce risks of failure and collapse; fill vacuums; raise the quality of public policy making; and employ multiple checks and balances as safety devices, energizers, democratizers and coordinators. Finally, these multipurpose organizations spread limited resources and talents and reinforce the community without imposing uniformity. The whole relies on self-initiative, mutual trust, reliable information, interdependence and interest coalition, all of which feed on turbulence.

SUMMARY OF CHARACTERISTICS

The administrative style imposed by crisis in Israe can be summarized through these precepts:

1. Organize resources so they can be mobilized instantly for emergency action, even if this entails bot underemployment in reserve areas and multiple interlocking office-holding. Unless payments can be delayed, avoid overcommitment in large-scale projects which cannot be halted or revised.

2. Organize talent to concentrate on key problems as they arise, accepting such difficulties as the rapid circulation of elites, temporary organizations and ambig uous position titles.

3. Concentrate on flexible leadership able to cros disciplinary and problem barriers, deal with diversity and variety, and think constructively on national issues

4. Stick to practical realities: leave speculatio and philosophizing for later.

5. Forget perfection and history's judgment--act and act quickly. Do not repeat past mistakes or brood over them.

6. Don't be irrevocably committed. Leave room to maneuver out of every situation. Preserve the element o surprise. This gains time or turns back the opposing initiative.

7. Maximize self-expression and self-reliance and personal initiative. Delegate.

8. Treat every problem separately and seek specifi solutions. Avoid imitation, standardization and uniformity.

9. Keep information moving and communications open

10. Give the appearance of normality at all times.
Don't panic.

The overall result is one of variety and confusion, not
of randomness. Anyone accustomed to smoothness or uniformity would wonder how anything could get done. But
results indicate it does, after a fashion.

This description of Israeli administrative culture
contains many elements common to other cultures facing
rapid change. In all these societies, the "givens" are
not quite what they seem to be; they change from one
moment to another. Because they do not conform to
rational models based on stability, these elements have
been ignored or viewed as dysfunctions. In fact, however, they are mechanisms and processes which enable the
administrative culture to undertake dynamic action and
continuous problem solving.

DEVELOPMENT CAPACITY

In the contemporary world, as specialization of
roles and fragmentation of functions proceed, a major
function of the administrative culture is to head off
problems by anticipating them, presenting alternative
strategies, and implementing selected solutions. Scientific management has developed tools to aid administrators in this task, but they are not as yet applicable to
large-scale complex problems with many unknowns. That
they are not sufficiently used is an indictment of the
administrative culture which is either unaware of their
existence or fails to train sufficient people to apply
them. Here Israel is at fault. Though the tools of
scientific management are employed in high priority
areas, there is still a tendency to rely on crusading
leadership to devise optimum solutions. In short,
ability to run the state as if it were an enlarged conspiratorial movement cannot meet continuing problems.
Low level problems command the attention of many with
talent and practical experience. Scientific management
would permit them to concentrate on the larger problems
that require central direction.

Each society has problems peculiar to itself; each must devise solutions that best meet its special circumstances. Blind imitation may prove costly. It may be the wrong solution; the right solution wrongly applied; or a temporary solution that intensifies the problem or pushes lasting solutions into the future. The symbols of progress in one society should not be confused with the substance of progress itself. Management science tools are symbols of administrative progress, but they do not constitute development capacity.

> The concept of development is process rather than content oriented and is on that basis to be distinguished from the concept of modernization. Development refers to the interactional process through which individuals associated in unit networks learn how to articulate and solve problems. Modernization refers to those symbols, products and modes of life associated with modernity...which a unit or its members may acquire.... Development...would refer to the rate at which problem-solving capacity was increasing or decreasing, while...modernization... would refer to the rate at which symbolic content was being accreted.[1]

Development, according to Biller, is not a manifest behavior like performance, but a latent learning process, a capacity to learn from problem solving. It is a process-oriented idea that "places more emphasis on what

---

[1]Robert P. Biller, "Some Implications of Adaptation Capacity for Organizational and Political Development," presented to the Minnowbrook Conference on the New Public Administration, September 1968. To be published as part of the conference proceedings by Syracuse University Press.

a unit is learning how to do through solving problems than on its symbols of modernity."[2]

Adopting Biller's approach, development capacity can be divided into the following sets of abilities:

1. The ability to recognize new problems that require new solutions rather than modifications of old solutions.

2. The ability to reformulate problems in new terms to elicit new responses and initiatives.

3. The ability to tolerate deviation, conflict and confrontation without overreacting or losing a sense of proportion.

4. The ability to turn crisis to advantage, to use deviation and conflict in problem solving so as to generate self-transformation with minimal alienation.

5. The ability to deal with uncertainty, fluidity, movement and turbulence; the capacity to absorb change, instability and interdependence.

6. The ability to mobilize resources to meet problems and to engage in multidisciplinary problem solving.

7. The ability to encourage error correction, initiative and creativity, and to learn from mistakes.

8. The ability to learn how to learn from experience and uncertainty.

9. The ability to pass on learning experience that is interactional, rather than content skills.

10. The ability to remain human, to keep a hold on fundamentals, to retain compassion, to acknowledge fallibility, and to laugh at one's own seriousness.

---

[2]Ibid., p. 23.

From what has already been said, it may be conclud
that Israel is well on the way to building development
capacity. Jews have survived as a nation for 2000 year
without a homeland. Their connection with Palestine wa
preserved in religious practices that repeatedly expres
ed hope of returning to the Promised Land. They have
faced persecution, slaughter, assimilation and disappea
ance. Yet somehow a remnant survived here and there, a
the line was continued, evidence enough of an amazing
capacity for resilience. Israel is carrying on that tr
dition.

CULTURAL ELEMENTS

Several cultural elements can be discerned in
Jewish-Israeli development capacity. *First*, the Jews
believe in the future: they are basically optimistic.
They may look back on a golden past, but they also awai
the dawn of the millennium that will end Jewish persecu
tion forever. They have great faith in themselves to
overcome adversity: somehow they will pull through,
crisis will create leaders and ideas, the slightest
chance will be seized. Having a homeland once again ha
made a great difference. They now have something on
which to build, something tangible that can be dis-
played, something they cannot afford to lose without
seriously harming their basic optimism. For Diaspora
Jewry, Israel represents an escape route, to be used if
things become as bad as they were at the height of anti-
Semitism. For Zionists, Israel must succeed, or life
will lose much of its meaning. For Israelis, there is
no alternative.

Second, the Jews have learned to live with their
problems by converting necessity into an ideal. Sometimes the ideal lives on long after the original necessity has passed. For example, Zionist labor pioneers
glorified the virtues of physical labor, but once mech-
anization was adopted, physical labor for its own sake
lost its appeal. Similarly, the wandering Jews had
little attachment to heavy goods or property. They

wanted nothing that could not be carried easily whenever they had to move on. Material comforts had to be sacrificed to preserve their lives, culture, religion and future as a nation. Thus poverty and deprivation were accepted, and frugality became a virtue. Greed only attracted attention, jealousy and covetousness; affluence was positively harmful unless it could buy off trouble, which it never did for long. The Zionist pioneers brought these values with them, and, aided by external danger, military sacrifices, Arab intransigence and low living standards idealized them on a communitywide scale. When the nature of problems changes--from poverty to affluence, or from insecurity to permanent peace-- changing social values will create new problems, and these will be idealized, just as the old problems were. They will not be ignored or condemned, but accepted for the challenge they present.

Third, Israelis have a remarkable capacity for adapting to change, be it new weapons systems or technological advances. The pace of change is furious, as if Israelis were trying to make up for centuries of lost time and neglect. Absorption continues apace, and the economy expands, aided by creativity and innovation. Israelis do not choose the obvious strategy; they have a flair for the novel and unexpected, reflecting personal initiative, improvisation and scholastic research.

There are, however, blocks that reduce adaptive capacity. First, the non-bureaucratic traditionalist groups change more slowly than others, if at all. How long they will survive, isolated by their inflexibility, is anybody's guess. They already have centuries of inertia behind them. Second, the older generations, growing tired of perpetual change, maintain the values that have served them well in the past. Finally, those who attain their goals early do not want to have the fruits of success snatched from them, nor do they want to move on to other fields where risks are higher. They have lost their sense of adventure, and are unresponsive until provoked. They have withdrawn from the process of perpetual self-transformation.

Fourth, in a coalition, compromise is unavoidable. Tolerance is reinforced by the presence of unassimilated minorities, the strength of individualism, external pressures and a strong belief in civil liberties. Turbulence is contained within a stable framework that prevents excess and channels efforts in purposive directions. Consensus is lacking, except on major issues, but it is compensated for by a fairly even division of contending forces, a low level of violence, the avoidance of direct confrontation, strict laws fairly and intelligently applied and preoccupation with problems of everyday living.

Fifth, Israelis have preferred to learn from their own experience. How much has been learned is hard to judge. Certainly the worst mistakes and excesses of the early years have not been repeated. Israelis have grown more prudent, and they try not to be caught twice in the same error. Learning how to learn is encouraged by both the youthful image projected at home and abroad and the delegation of responsibility to young people, but it is diminished by the tendency of elderly leaders to hang onto public office without training qualified successors.

Sixth, Israelis are great risk takers. Almost everything they do is a gamble, and so far most gambles have paid off. They accept the consequences of gambling the disasters as well as the rewards. The strain and excitement of the daily struggle for existence is reflected in leisure activities--entertaining, excursions, cultural pursuits, cinema and just plain relaxation. There is little emphasis on such artificial stimulants as professional sport, alcohol, drugs, vice, games of chance (with the exception of the national lottery) and night clubs.

None of these six elements is easily transferable. The recipe is difficult to duplicate. Mix up 50 different ethnic backgrounds, add fear of extermination, stir in theological disputes, heat up over centuries of rootlessness and persecution, and allow to simmer in hostile surroundings, and the end product may still bear no resemblance to the Israeli model.

CHAPTER XII

The Significance of
Israeli Administrative Culture

As no two situations are identical, generalizations drawn from a single case may be highly misleading. But although the specific combination of factors and circumstances in Israel may be unique, the component parts are not, and Israeli experiences may be illuminating to other nations caught in similar situations. Zionism is unique to the Jewish people and Israel, but Israeli methods for dealing with rapid change and crisis may be transferable to other new states confronted with similar sets of social problems.

At several points, we have questioned bureaucratic conceptions of administration. In such matters as centralized national planning, unifunctional organization, politicization, professionalism and budgeting, Israeli experience contradicts certain scientific management dicta. What can be learned from Israel's experience? What general principles apply to problems of developmental regimes? What significant conclusions can be drawn from the foregoing analysis of Israel's administrative culture?

PROBLEMS OF COMPARISON

The first and most obvious comment is that appearances are deceiving. No observer can be completely objective, for he is already preconditioned by his own culture, which creates images of what to expect. He tends to seek confirmation of his preconceptions and selects his material accordingly, usually from the superficial rather than the essential elements of the administrative culture. In Israel, the European will rarely find imposing public buildings with large majestic halls, statues of past heroes and brightly uniformed guards. The North American will find few glass and plastic palaces whose polished, antiseptic floors reflect bright fluorescent lighting, whose fast-moving elevators, central heating, air conditioning, automatic vending machines and piped music coddle the senses. The Asian will miss the large open-air gatherings of people waiting for services to be brought by mobile units.

Buildings, dress, machinery, the reception of visitors--these tell little about what really is accomplished. The observer may miss the essentials. He may fail to appreciate all the circumstances, all the different environmental factors, resources and social objectives that obtain in unfamiliar administrative cultures. To understand how things are done in a given situation, he must go behind the scenes and break through the mechanisms that distort reality.

An observer like de Tocqueville may acclimatize himself in a few weeks. In a short time, he understands the new culture better than many natives who have spent their lives in it, never quite knowing what it is or how its administrative culture operates. Perhaps anyone who wants to understand his own culture better must spend some time outside. The resulting comparisons and contrasts may clarify reality and lead to questioning of both values and institutional forms.

Using concepts developed in foreign administrative cultures, it is easy to condemn Israeli institutional patterns, administrative behavior and organizational norms. Indeed, until he learns to appreciate the rules of the Israeli administrative game, this is the newcomer's instinctive reaction. The organizational structure of the governmental subsystem is functionally irrational. Staff serving the public directly are often incompetent, rude, aggressive and indifferent. In adverse weather, services break down. Plans are overruled, shelved, ignored, by-passed and discontinued under group pressures. Salary administration, job classification and tax regulations are virtually incomprehensible. Trade unions usurp management functions. Inspection is inadequate and badly performed. In a functionary's absence, his work piles up and is not divided among other staff. The staff is of poor quality, and its members work slowly; low work norms are protected by powerful employee organizations. The list of faults could be extended.[1] Further, these faults have serious consequences. For instance, inattention to legally required safety precautions, combined with employee carelessness, has resulted in the unnecessary destruction of expensive plant and loss of human life.

No conspiracy of silence hides these shortcomings in Israeli administration; administrative critics gain ample publicity in the mass media. Israelis do not need to be reminded of bad performance. They are more interested in prescriptions for reform which consider both their unique environmental factors, resources and social objectives, and the sacrifices entailed in improving administrative performance.

Discussions with a wide range of Israeli administrators indicate that they are not optimistic about

---

[1] See for instance Edwin Samuel, "Efficiency in the Israel Civil Service," *Canadian Public Administration*, 4(2): 191-196 (1961).

prospects for administrative reform.[2] They argue that perfection is unattainable; that there will always be cause for criticism; and that progress will inevitably differ among individuals, units, organizations and subsystems. Since they themselves are the principal losers, they are doing what they can to improve performance. Foreign prescriptions have been tried and found wanting. In their own assessment, they are not doing badly. They see no guarantee that radical reforms will work, that new accommodations will guarantee increased productivity, that open competitive examinations will improve entry standards, or orthodox budgeting reduce scandals. They claim that reform is not a question of adjusting this or that superficial component; it demands wholesale changes in such major cultural features as personal insecurity, national paranoia, pride, missionary zeal, individualism and optimism.

ADMINISTRATIVE AND PARENT CULTURES

The interdependence of the administrative culture and its parent culture does not diminish with differentiation, specialization and fragmentation. The unity of knowledge remains intact. Professionalization of specialists tends to downgrade generalists. Thus as specialists are caught up in the excitement of new discoveries about the inner workings of a system, more of the external relationships of the system are simply assumed. In administrative science, the distorting effects of specialization are being counteracted by comparative studies of administration. The studies

---

[2]Discussions were conducted at the Central School of Administration, Public Administration Annual Conferences, Israel Management Center Seminars and with administrators in a wide range of organizations. Some of the comments recorded here are contained in *Administrative Reform in Israel* (Hebrew), a Report by a Select Committee, Central School of Administration, Ramat Rachel, Jerusalem, 1967.

emphasize (1) integration of administrative subsystems, (2) integration of organizational and administrative theory, and (3) integration of administrative and social theory.

In Israel, administrative reform is dependent on social reform, as the practitioners argue. Significant changes in the administrative culture would need to be preceded or accompanied by a number of other changes including

1. changes in the composition and outlook of the political elite to ensure a higher priority for administration;

2. overhaul of the educational system that would have to devote more resources to administrative studies and increase contacts between practitioners and educators;

3. shifts in social mores that permit tolerance of inefficiency, featherbedding, overprotective unionism and restrictive practices; and

4. reduction of vested interests in fragmentation by incentives to amalgamate, compulsory rationalization, and by opposition to discrimination in any form.

In turn, administrative reform would promote social reform. The unification or nationalization of private health insurance would end discrimination against excluded groups. Stricter penalties on misuse of public funds and enforcement of orthodox financing would raise the image of the governmental subsystems; block some existing paths to corruption; end unequal tax burdens, illegal privileges and maldistribution of real income; and raise the morale of the underprivileged, who are resentful of recurrent scandals. Greater efficiency would improve productivity, release savings for other purposes and raise the standard of living. Profound social ramifications would, for example, follow a reduction in the six-day workweek.

LACK OF ADMINISTRATIVE SPECIALIZATION

Distinctions between administrative subsystems in Israel are blurred because the country is on a permanent war footing and because indispensable capital imports are largely channeled through a governmental apparatus that includes all political movements, except the very extremes. The public rarely differentiates among subsystems in its expectations and complaints: it is unlikely that most citizens could even tell the subtle differences between mixed enterprises and joint ventures. Strong national trade unions endeavor to treat all employers alike, subject to internal political pressures. The mobility of administrators between subsystems also suggests a degree of universalism in the administrative culture.

The key area is the governmental bureaucracy. It could effectively dominate other subsystems, but is prevented from doing so by antistatist ideologies, external pressure from private donors, and distrust of public authority. Formally, the public bureaucracy unifies the whole culture through contacts with the World Zionist movement and the Jewish Agency (and hence Diaspora Jewry), direct controls over the public sector, indirect controls over the private sector and mixed enterprises, ties with voluntary associations and responsibility for the Israel Defense Forces and local governments. No aspect of public life is immune from the governmental bureaucracy. No other subsystem is in such a commanding position or overlaps so extensively with other subsystems.

It is not the legal status of activities but their political importance that determines the strength of formal links and central direction. In high priority areas, such as security and essential communications, the links are strong and are reinforced by stronger informal ties. In low priority areas, the governmental bureaucracy rarely intervenes more than is necessary to protect the public interest; participants do not encourage

governmental interference and prefer partisan mutual
adjustment. Thus a private enterprise carrying out a
high priority activity is more bound to public policy
and governmental controls than is a public enterprise
or governmental unit carrying out a low priority
activity. Similarly, a border *kibbutz* settlement is tied
more closely to the government than is another *kibbutz*
belonging to the same political movement but located away
from the borders.

Naturally, subsystems operate differently according
to function, type of organization, size of activities,
social objectives, status and staff mores. *Kibbutzim* are
run on different lines from *moshavim*; the management of
large-scale Histadrut development enterprises constrasts
sharply with that of small entrepreneurial entities.
Given the diversity of administrative styles, the range
of administrative behavior may be wider than that of the
United States and the Soviet Union, even though Israel is
smaller and subsystem identification correspondingly more
difficult. Perhaps this is a feature of all developmental regimes in which the different aspects of social
development are merged. Perhaps the barriers among the
subdisciplines of administrative science need to be over-
hauled.

ORGANIZATIONAL RIGIDITY

Israeli institutional forms are less important than
administrative styles. Organizational rigidity has been
marked since 1952. There are now more organizations, and
the larger ones have diversified internally, but no star-
tling innovations have occurred. The cumulative costs of
rigidity are approaching the level where, despite adverse
circumstances, it becomes worthwhile to undergo the disruption and enmity that accompany large-scale reorganization. Organizational rigidity is largely responsible for
the continuation of bureaupathology. The kind of control
administration built into many organizations cannot adequately accommodate the demands of adaptive administration. Nor can it incorporate the more advanced forms
made possible by new technologies.

Israel would score well on Thompson's developmental requisites.[3] It features an innovative atmosphere, operationalized and widely shared planning goals (major social objectives), integration of planning (thinking) and action (doing), a cosmopolitan atmosphere, diffusion of influence, increasing tolerance of interdependency, an avoidance of bureaupathology. But organizational rigidity prevents the reshaping of problems, rational decision processes (as against political bargaining), decentralization, participative decisionmaking, adequate feedback and creativity. Administrators have had to get around institutionalized barriers by developing extensive informal networks, joint projects, temporary organizations, methods of evading rules (to the point of blatant hypocrisy), *protekzia*, middlemen (fixers, troubleshooters, informers), staff rotation and other adaptive devices. In short, administrators accept the framework and adjust to it, rather than altering it to better meet changing needs. It is easier to arrange things informally than to undergo the expense and trouble of formal confrontations which stir emotions among a wider audience.

INDIVIDUALS AND INNOVATION

The key people in Israel are those who can work systems and make systems work. It is individuals, not groups, classes or organizations who provide creativity, push innovations, persuade sceptics and critics, obtain general approval, search for resources, advise on implementation, teach colleagues, check operations, and do the hundred and one other things necessary to change existing systems. It is individual endeavor, supported by allies and opposed by rivals, conservatives, indifferents and perfectionists, that provides the energy. It is individuals who are fired by a total commitment to

---

[3]V.A. Thompson, "Administrative Objectives for Development Administration," *Administrative Science Quarterly*, 9(1): 91-108 (1964).

Israel, mobilized by mass movements and sought by charismatic leaders. Their motives, like their origins, are varied, but they survive only so long as they succeed. They are not defined by family, party, residence, wealth, club or other ascriptive criteria, but by their ability to manipulate systems and their recognition of similar ability in others. They are not yet organization men but energizers who activate bureaucrats and technocrats. They are self-made leaders. They cannot always articulate why they are what they are. Because of this, they are sceptical of scientific management unless it proves itself in operation. They leave theorizing to professors.

These crusading managers (the energizers) now wear the pioneering mantle of the Second Aliyah, for they most resemble the pushing, hard working, dynamic *chuzpahdic* (cheeky) *sabra* image. Some are grey haired or balding men in baggy shorts; others are open necked, short sleeved, white shirted middle managers; still another group are well groomed, immaculately dressed executives. They seem impervious to complaint, except from one another. To reach their current positions, they had to be thickskinned, although when their defenses are breached by persons they respect, they react sharply.

On the other hand, they are reluctant to acknowledge the wisdom of the common man, or the "where-the-shoe-pinches" aspect of democracy. This makes them appear haughty and autocratic. But the energizers have had to live with criticism all their lives, much of it unfounded, unjust and malicious. They have been maligned by Diaspora Jewry, members of different *Aliyot*, political opponents and many more. Endemic criticism and complaint spring from comparisons with wealthy Diaspora Jewry, with better conditions experienced outside Israel, with images of how Israeli elites live, or with personal conceptions of what ought to be. Complaints express both dissatisfaction with the status quo and expectation of continuous improvement. Whatever the crusading managers do, someone will say it is wrong; no matter how well they perform, they cannot please everybody. So the crusading managers have learned to live with criticisms, mainly by ignoring them. Consequently, the volume of dissent is a less reliable guide to performance in Israel than it might be elsewhere. Ignored altogether by impregnable elites and cocksure adventurists, criticism tends to feed on itself Emergencies, however, restore a sense of balance.

Most criticism occurs in less important areas, including clientele services. These naturally receive the greatest attention, being close to the public, universal and obvious. Much of the criticism is exaggerated, repetitious, or a hangover from earlier days when conditions were worse. Many factors fail to receive ade quate consideration: efficacious performance in high priority areas, high standards of performance in less publicized activities, handicaps imposed by the politico military situation, low quality resources and the impossibly high standards of comparison.

Paradoxically, Israel has been comparatively successful because, lacking the latest modernization symbols, it had to improvise in many areas. This generated creativity and originality and tapped a self-sacrificing dynamism that carried the country through crisis after crisis, problem after problem. The fact that Israel has had to make its own way under adverse conditions has beer its greatest asset. Instead of relying on foreign aid tc provide administrative and technical know-how, Israel had to develop them for itself. Now it has entered the take-off stage, and can progress through its own internal momentum. But the full depth and extent of Israel's develop opment capacity have yet to be tested. So far, the administrative culture has risen to every challenge. Adversity has been turned to advantage, handicaps to assets, defeats to victories (and occasionally vice versa). The administrative culture may well need crisis, external threats, internal divisions and insecurity in order to maintain its development capacity. Relaxation of tension may release resources from innovative problem solving and transfer them to consolidation of bureaucratism.

PROBLEMS OF EVALUATION

One problem that has arisen repeatedly in analyzing Israel's administrative culture has been assessment and evaluation. Although there are no firm guidelines yet, some pointers can be suggested. First, there are the standards of universal conduct derived from the best moral teachings and from the hopes and ambitions of the common man. Does the administrative culture preserve "life, liberty and the pursuit of happiness"? "Liberté, égalité, and fraternité"? Does it uphold the United Nations Covenant of Civil and Political Rights? Conserve irreplaceable natural beauties? At present, such ideals are expressed simply in slogans: these must be transformed into specific acts before meaningful assessment can be undertaken.

Second, at the other end of the scale, evaluation could begin with low level administrative subsystems. If each subsystem achieved its objectives, maintained internal stability and adapted to its changing environment, it could be assumed that whole administrative systems and cultures were performing well. Guideline assessments at the subsystem level already exist: productivity, economy, efficiency, organizational effectiveness, bureaucratization, high quality decisionmaking, ability to handle crisis and clientele and staff satisfaction. Scientific management tools are readily available for concrete assessments.

These two methods of assessment would not, however, answer such questions as: What administrative arrangements best promote the flow of human knowledge and enable leaders to assimilate new knowledge as soon as it becomes available? What is the most effective method of organizing information and communications to induce transformation of human values? How can institutional deficiencies be discovered and rectified with the minimum of dislocation? How does administrative behavior detract from social ends, and to what extent can administration be minimized in the conduct of human affairs?

These questions are germane to the nature and performance of administrative cultures as they contribute to social objectives. They raise issues perceived only dimly by the pioneers of scientific management, men who naively thought that better administrative performance alone would solve the human predicament, that higher productivity would alleviate human frustration. A prosperous economy and happy work relationships may well be ingredients of the good society, but they are not necessarily the most important. The highest standards of administrative performance may not prevent catastrophe if the parent culture is destructive; if the world order is unable to prevent collisions among different cultures.

Lack of progress in performance evaluation and measurement, even at low levels, is due in part to a certain reluctance to expend resources on completed activities. The fruits of the study are, after all, mainly academic or historical. Evaluation is justified if it throws light on present events or activities or, even better, if it helps anticipate the future. But conditions change so rapidly that even the most sophisticated projective techniques are little better than the inspired guesswork of science fiction. People are not anxious to learn from a past that bears little resemblance to the present or the future. Nor are they concerned with the judgment of history when they are striving to do the best they can with the knowledge at hand.

Measurement can, in fact, be dysfunctional. It diverts resources from current tasks, but does not contribute to problem solving. By belittling the unmeasureable, it distorts perception. The confirmation of good performance may lead to complacency, while confirmation of bad performance may be self-incriminating. For the purposes of security and reassurance, ignorance may be bliss. Who really wants the truth? Long before modern psychology, charismatic leaders discovered that people hear only what they want to hear, believe only what they want to believe. Harbingers of truth--prophets, academics, scientists--have not always been welcomed by their own kind, let alone by the uninitiated. Civilizations strive to disguise the truth about themselves and dictatorships are not the only regimes that reinterpret history in their own image.

Even if the psychological obstacles were overcome, practical difficulties would continue to handicap evaluation. There is no agreement about what to measure. No two authors agree on how, precisely, to distinguish administration from other social activities. Throughout much of the short history of administrative science, the predominant concern has been the study of how to attain given social goals and, in the process, how to fulfill such intermediate administrative goals as orderliness, intelligent utilization of human and material resources, elimination of waste and inefficiency, economy, employee welfare, satisfaction of clientele, anticipation and resolution of problems, provision of guidance and others. Lately, the management sciences have discovered that the method selected helps determine social goals; comparative administration studies have indicated that concentration on means is a culture-bound approach which fails to relate the administrative culture to its unique environment. In short, administration is more than the "nuts and bolts" of social organization.

Administrative performance is related to the parent culture, its exchange values and transformatory processes, its social milieu and place in the world order and its stage in administrative development. But who best understands an administrative culture--the insider who is a product of that culture or the more objective outsider? How can the superior resources, political power and propaganda appeal of a leading state be discounted when reviewing the administrative capabilities of one of its dependencies? How is Weber's appraisal of the merits of legal-rational authority to be weighed against liberal criticism of bureaupathology? Or against the controversies surrounding wartime atrocities, particularly the bureaucratic system of mass murder at issue during the Eichmann trial? How do large-scale economies compensate for reduced competition, loss in personal interdependence and initiative, and employee and clientele alienation? Even if these and other questions are answered satisfactorily, shifts in the cultural milieu--in social mores, technology, education and health standards, religious beliefs, physical mobility--make time comparisons hazardous.

Ideally, an evaluator would seek to assess the performance of an administrative culture in three ways: first, in terms of its own social values and environmental limitations; second, in terms of his own culture, where this was markedly different; and third, in terms of the values of a transcendental perfect society. Such assessments are made by administrative reformers seeking to raise existing performance, by overseas experts advising on performance in terms of their own values, and by social revolutionaries who measure the present in terms of a preconceived future society.

While each of these groups contains culture-bound and pedantic individuals, there is increasing recognition that evaluation of administration cannot be divorced from its wider context and that interrelationships are so complex as to defy exact quantification. Data processing mechanisms may improve man's capacity to deal with variety, but they cannot as yet determine the relative importance of administrative performance (higher or lower staff morale, improved decisionmaking, utilization of spare capacity, better appearance of the product) as opposed to other factors (technological innovation, better trained employees, lower absenteeism resulting from the prevention of epidemics and public disturbances, speculation, better appeal of the product, sunny weather, astrology, sunspots). At best, then, evaluations are tendency measures, even though at low levels they may be susceptible to a high degree of quantification.

These problems are accentuated in assessing the performance of the administrative culture of a new state. Particularly in the major centers of settlement, the inherited administrative system combines features of a traditional culture undergoing rapid modernization with those of an imported culture previously superimposed, but now freely accepted by new elites. The uneasy coexistence of old and new, neither fused nor fully differentiated but "prismatic," makes for peculiar hybrids that defy simple classification.

The tension between administrative styles and the organizations which embody them threatens to erupt into bitter conflict accompanied by emotional outpourings and physical violence. In this situation, public revelations of inner strife are academic luxuries that cannot be afforded. Researchers may be discouraged altogether, limited to relatively safe areas, or allowed to publish only constructive remarks--to a select audience. Conscious of failure and shortcomings, bureaucratic elites do not want outside harassment, imitative solutions, or publicity focusing on poor performance. They want favorable publicity or none at all. They want their praises sung, their successes applauded, their plans and remedial actions publicized. In this, they are supported by those nationalists who resent criticism of their homeland outside their own closed circle. In any event, there is insufficient information for meaningful analysis. And no matter how badly the administrative culture may be failing the country, there is no ready substitute. For lack of any practical alternative, researchers must rely on haphazard information, inspired guesswork and tendency measures, all highly controversial because of their subjectivity.

Without minimizing the problems--disagreement over definitions, scope and identification, absence of guidelines, unsuitability of the universal absolutes and criteria employed at lower levels, multiplicity of issues, inadequacy of data, practical difficulties and psychological blocks--an examination of Israel's administrative culture suggests that the attempt to assess an entire national administrative system can be rewarding. Some traditional approaches are inadequate and misleading, for they fail to reveal the essence of Israeli dynamism and concentrate unduly on fashionable symbols. Reversing the process, it is seen that Israel possesses certain factors that may compensate for deficiencies in resources, education, technology, capital and know-how. In the long run, these factors may be an important basis for continuing development. If so, how can such factors be successfully introduced into hostile environments?

Bibliographic Notes

For a new state, Israel has accumulated a sizable
literature, but much of it is only vaguely related to
the nation's administrative culture. The most scholarly
introduction is that of S.N. Eisenstadt, *Israeli Society*
(London: Weidenfeld and Nicholson, 1967). This work is
more up to date than most and contains a comprehensive
bibliography. The emphasis is largely sociological and
while the book contains a mass of material, it is not
easy to read: parts resemble a poorly arranged collection of competent research reports, inadequately integrated.

It may be easier to begin with any one of a number
of sympathetic overviews: A.J. Heschel, *Israel: An Echo
of Eternity* (New York: Farrar, Straus and Giroux, 1969);
Terence Prittie, *Israel: Miracle in the Desert* (New
York: Praeger, 1967); Donald B. Robinson, *Under Fire:
Israel's Twenty Year Struggle for Survival* (New York:
Norton, 1968); Robert S. Gamzey, *Miracle of Israel* (New
York: Herzl Press, 1965); G. Ashe, *The Land and the Book:
Israel the Perennial Nation* (London: Collins, 1965);
Ruth Gruber, *Israel Today: Land of Many Nations* (New
York: Hill and Wang, 1963); D. Elston, *No Alternative:*

Israel Observed (London: Hutchinson, 1960); Norman Bentwich, *Israel Resurgent* (New York: Praeger, 1960); Kurt Schubert, *Israel: State of Hope* (Stuttgart: Schworben Verlag, 1960); Irving Miller, *Israel--The Eternal Idea* (New York: Farrar, Straus and Cudahy, 1955) and David Ben-Gurion, *Rebirth and Destiny of Israel* (New York: Philosophical Library, Inc., 1954).

Among the current English periodicals that frequently contain articles relevant to Israel's administrative culture are *Commentary* (New York), *The Middle East Journal* (Washington, D.C.), *Jewish Observer* (London), *New Outlook* (Tel Aviv), and *The Jerusalem Post*

The administrative legacy of Israel can be gleaned from several sources. The new state's identification with the past can be seen in its keen interest in archaeology, best illustrated in Yigael Yadin, *Masada: Herod's Fortress and the Zealots' Last Stand* (New York: Random House, 1967); Ronald Sanders, *Israel: The View from Masada* (New York: Harper and Row, 1966); Moshe Pearlman and Yaakov Yanna, *Historical Sites in Israel* (New York: Vanguard Press, 1965); and Yigael Yadin, *The Art of Warfare in Biblical Lands* (New York: McGraw-Hill, 1963).

The Spirit of Zionism and the Yishuv is best exemplified ideologically in Arthur Hertzberg, ed., *The Zionist Idea: A Historical Analysis and Reader* (New York: Doubleday and Herzl Press, 1959); and Ben Halpern, *The Idea of the Jewish State* (Cambridge, Mass.: Harvard University Press, 1961). Empirical examples include J. Ophir, *The National Worker Book: History of the National Workers' Movement in Palestine* (Hebrew) (Tel Aviv: The General Labor Organization Executive Committee, vols. for 1958-1959); M. Breslavski, *The Jewish Workers' Movement in Palestine* (Hebrew) (Tel Aviv: Hakibbutz Hameuchal, vols. for 1959-1963); Z. Rosenstein, *History of the Workers' Movement in Palestine* (Hebrew) (Tel Aviv: Am Oved, vols. for 1958-1964); Harry Viteles, *A History of the Cooperative Movement in Israel: A Source Book* (London: Vallentine-Mitchell, 1967); and Munya M. Mardor, *Haganah* (New York: New American Library, 1966).

The Archives of Israel, Prime Minister's Office, Jerusalem; the Archives of the Jewish Agency, also in Jerusalem; historical records preserved by the major political parties, mainly in Tel Aviv; the Histadrut records, located in Tel Aviv; and local government records preserved in Jerusalem and in long established settlements, all contain valuable source materials which have been little used so far.

Different perspectives can be found in the Turkish records scattered in Istanbul; some British records preserved in London; and remnants of the Arab community records in Jerusalem, Amman and Gaza. Especially helpful are Bernard Joseph, *British Rule in Palestine* (Washington, D.C.: Public Affairs Press, 1948); Robert H. Drayton, *Laws, Statutes...of Palestine* (London: Waterlow and Sons, 1934); the *Official Gazette of the Government of Palestine* (later *Palestine Gazette*) (1920-1938); and *Palestine Law Reports*.

The problems of transition were dealt with at the time in a flood of romantic literature. Less emotional are Zeev Sherf, *Three Days* (London: W.H. Allen, 1962) and Edwin Samuel, *Problems of Government in the State of Israel* (Jerusalem: Rubin Mass, 1956). Both touch on continuing problems such as defense, immigrant absorption, party rivalry, religion, education and more importantly, governmental arrangements, public finance and civil service. The governmental transition is covered in Z. Rosen, "The Structure and Machinery of the State" in *Be Terem* (Tel Aviv: September 1948); and Hal Lehrman, "The Israelis Learn to Govern Themselves: Politics and Polticians in the New State," *Commentary*, 10-19 (July 1949).

Social arrangements in Israel are covered in a number of publications including: S.N. Eisenstadt, "The Social Structure of Israel" in Arnold M. Rose, ed., *The Institutions of Advanced Societies* (Minneapolis: University of Minnesota Press, 1958); S.N. Eisenstadt, H. Adler, R. Bar-Yosef and R. Kahane, *The Social Structure of Israel* (Hebrew) (Jerusalem: Akademon, 1966) and

Edwin Samuel, *The Structure of Society in Israel* (New York: Random House, 1969). Social values are discussed by S.N. Eisenstadt, "Israel: Traditional and Modern Social Values and Economic Development," *Annals...American Academy of Political and Social Science* (May 1956); Judah Matras, *Social Change in Israel* (Chicago: Aldine, 1965); Alex Weingrod, *Israel: Group Relations in a New Society* (London: Pall Mall Press, 1965); and, more critically, by I. Kanev, *Social Policy in Israel* (Tel Aviv: Social Research Institute, 1964).

Immigration and absorption have received attention in S.N. Eisenstadt, *The Absorption of Immigrants* (London: Routledge and Kegan Paul, 1954); Myrna Sikron, *The Immigration to Israel 1948-1953* (Jerusalem: Falk Institute and Central Bureau of Statistics, 1957); Judith T. Shuval, *Immigrants on the Threshold* (New York: Atherton Press, 1963); and Alex Weingrod, *Reluctant Pioneers* (Ithaca: Cornell University Press, 1966). The problems of social integration are also examined by S.N. Eisenstadt, "The Oriental Jews in Israel," *Jewish Social Studies*, 12 (1950); Judith T. Shuval, "Emerging Patterns of Ethnic Strain in Israel," *Social Forces*, 40(4): 323-330 (1962); and Abraham A. Weinberg, *Migration and Belonging: A Study of Mental Health and Personal Adjustment in Israel* (The Hague: M. Nijholf, Studies in Social Life, No. 5, 1961). The position of the Arab minorities in Israel is reviewed in Walter Schwarz, *The Arabs in Israel* (London: Faber, 1959); Abner Cohen, *Arab Border Villages in Israel: a Study of Continuity and Change in Social Organization* (Manchester University Press, 1965); and Emanuel Marx, *Bedouin of the Negev* (Manchester University Press, 1967).

More specialized is Jacob M. Landau, *The Arabs in Israel: A Political Study* (London: Oxford University Press, 1969). The educational system is described in Randolph L. Braham, *Israel: A Modern Education System* (Washington, D.C.: United States Department of Health, Education, and Welfare, 1966); Joseph S. Bentwich, *Education in Israel* (London: Routledge and Kegan Paul, 1965); and H. Merhavia, *The Educational System in Israel* (Hebrew) (Jerusalem: Achiasaff, 1957).

Other social services are described in N. Baruch, *Major Problems of the Development of the Social Services 1965-1970* (Jerusalem: Ministry of Social Welfare, 1964) and the various publications of The Henrietta Szold Institute for Child and Youth Welfare, Jerusalem. Life in collectives and cooperatives is studied in Murray Weingarten, *Life in a Kibbutz* (New York: Reconstructionist Press, 1955); Aryei Fishman, *The Religious Kibbutz Movement: The Revival of the Jewish Religious Community* (Jerusalem: Jewish Agency, 1957); Melford E. Spiro, *Children of the Kibbutz* (Cambridge, Mass.: Harvard University Press, 1958); Haim Darin-Drabkin, *The Other Society* (New York: Harcourt, Brace and World, 1962); Albert I. Rabin, *Growing Up in the Kibbutz* (New York: Springer, 1965); and Bruno Bettelheim, *The Children of the Dream* (New York: Macmillan, 1969).

Literature devoted to the Israeli economy is somewhat sparse and has been overtaken by current events. Of historical interest are Don Patinkin, *The Israeli Economy: The First Decade* (Jerusalem: Falk Institute, 1960) and Alex Rubner, *The Economy of Israel* (New York: Praeger, 1960). Less dated is Ferdynand Zweig, *The Israeli Worker* (New York: Herzl Press and Sharon Books, 1959), which still offers a good insight into the Israeli labor scene. Both Edwin Samuel, "The Histadrut," *Political Quarterly*, 31(2): 176-184 (1960) and Ferdynand Zweig "The Jewish Trade Union Movement in Israel," *Jewish Journal of Sociology* (1959), need revision.

For current developments, the publications of the Bank of Israel and the Central Bureau of Statistics should be consulted, together with reports from the Ministries of Labor, Commerce and Industry, and Agriculture. Still relevant are A.G. Gaaton, "Economic Growth in Israel, 1948-1962" (Hebrew), *Liveon Lekalkala* 2(6) (1964); David Horowitz, *Economic Theory and Economic Policy in Israel* (Hebrew) (Tel Aviv: Am Oved, 1958); David Horowitz, *Structure and Trend in Israel's Economy* (Hebrew) (Tel Aviv: Masada, 1964); Michael Rozenburg, *The Measurement of the Economic Absorption of Israel's New Immigrant Sector from a National Point of View*

(Jerusalem: Kaplan School, Hebrew University, 1961); and
David Horowitz, *The Economics of Israel* (New York,
Pergamon: 1967). Economic institutions are reviewed by
U. Yadin, "The Public Corporation in Israel," in Wolfgar
Friedmann, ed., *The Public Corporation, A Comparative
Symposium* (Carswell, Toronto: 1954); A. Malkin, *The His-
tadrut Within the State* (Hebrew) (Beil Berel: Ovnaim,
1961); and N. Halevi and R. Klinov-Malul, *The Developmen
of the Israeli Economy* (Jerusalem: Bank of Israel, 1965)

Some interesting sidelights are provided by H.
Halperin, *Agrindus: Integration of Agriculture and In-
dustries* (London: Routledge and Kegan Paul, 1963) and
Raanan Weitz and Avshalom Rokach, *Agricultural Develop-
ment Planning and Implementation: An Israeli Case Study*
(New York: Praeger, 1968).

The administrative aspects of the polity are men-
tioned in brief in political science works. The changin
ideology of Israeli society is analyzed by A. Antonovsky
"Political Ideologies of Israelis" (Hebrew), *Amot*, 1: 21
28 (August-September 1963); A. Arian, "Voting and Ideology in Israel," *Midwest Journal of Political Science*,
10(3): 265-287 (August 1966); A. Arian, "Ideological
Change in Israel; a Study of Legislators, Civil Servants
and University Students," Ph.D. dissertation, Department
of Political Science, Michigan State University, 1965;
and Lester G. Seligman, *Leadership in a New Nation:
Political Development in Israel* (New York: Atherton
Press, 1964). The last is a survey of Knesset members'
opinions of the polity, perhaps reading too much into
the responses and overemphasizing the impact of Knesset
Members. Some change in emphasis can also be denoted in
Maurice Samuel, *Light in Israel* (New York: Knopf, 1968)
and in biographies of leading Israeli statesmen, as por-
trayed in Chaim Weizmann, *Trial and Error* (New York:
Schocken Press, 1966); B. Litvinoff, *Ben-Gurion of Israe.
(New York: Praeger, 1954); Michael Bar-Zohar, *Ben-Gurion.
The Armed Prophet* (New Jersey: Prentice-Hall, 1968);
Marie Syrkin, *Golda Meir, Woman With a Cause* (New
York: Putnam's, 1963); Terence Prittie, *Eshkol, The
Man and The Nation* (New York: Pitman, 1969); and

Naphtalie Lau-Levie, *Moshe Dayan, A Biography* (London:
Vallentine, Mitchell, 1968).

The earliest books on political science were heavily
legal and constitutional in emphasis. Still relevant is
Emanuel Rackman, *Israel's Emerging Constitution 1948-1951*
(New York: Columbia University Press, 1955). It has now
been largely superseded by the revised editions of
Yehoshua Freudenheim, *Government in Israel* (Hebrew),
translated into English by Meir Silverstone and Chaim I.
Goldwater, and published in Dobbs Ferry, New York by
Oceana Publications, 1967. The book contains chapters
on civil liberties, executive arrangements, legal system,
audit and legal controls and local government.

A shift in direction came with R. Roshwald, "Politi-
cal Parties and Social Classes in Israel," *Social
Research*, 23: 199-218 (Summer 1956); and Benjamin Akzin,
"The Role of Parties in Israeli Democracy," *The Journal
of Politics*, 17: 507-545 (November 1955). They preceded
the pioneering work on the formative years of the state,
Marver H. Bernstein, *The Politics of Israel: The First
Decade of Statehood* (Princeton University Press, 1957),
which still remains definitive, although out of date.
Bernstein's work is the most comprehensive analysis of
the formative years; it traces the administrative evolution of the State of Israel in detail, and captures the
feel of the 1950's. Particularly important are Chapters
6 to 13, which describe the administrative setting,
Israeli Civil Service, economic policy, budget making,
the State Comptroller, local government and the embryo
welfare state. Bernstein's essay, "Israel's Capacity to
Govern," *World Politics*, 11(3): 399-417 (1959), was further expanded in several directions by Israeli scholars
such as Amitai Etzioni, "Alternative Ways to Democracy:
The Example of Israel," *Political Science Quarterly*,
74(2): 196-216 (June 1959), which has been extensively
reproduced in several comparative politics readers,
and E. Gutmann, "The Development of Local Government in
Palestine," Ph.D. dissertation, Faculty of Political
Science, Columbia University, 1958; "Citizen Participation in Political Life in Israel," *International Social*

Science Journal, 12: 53-62 (1960); "Some Observations on Politics and Parties in Israel," *India Quarterly*, 18(1): 3-27 (January-March 1961); and "Israel," in R. Rose and A.J. Heidenheimer, eds., Comparative Political Finance, *Journal of Politics*, 25: 703-717 (1963).

Some of the new material was incorporated in O. Kraines, *Government and Politics in Israel* (Boston: Houghton Mifflin, 1961), a rather traditional work that concentrates on institutions. It includes a bibliography. The Kraines book covered much the same ground as previous works, but Chapters 10 to 12 concerning civil liberties, governmental administration and local government, had something new to say. A good companion piece is Yehezkel Dror and E. Gutmann, eds., *The Government of Israel* (Jerusalem: Akademon, 1961), a collection of constitutional documents. A different perspective, now revised to take account of the Six Day War, has recently been provided by Leonard J. Fein, *Israel: Politics and People*, rev. ed. (Boston: Little, Brown and Co., 1968), which corrected several errors of fact and emphasis in the earlier edition. From the administrative viewpoint, Chapter 5 on power centers (pp. 196-260) is most relevant.

The institutional tradition has been continued by M. Rossetti, *The Knesset: Its Origin, Form and Procedures* (Jerusalem: 1966), now superseded by Asher Zidon, *Knesset--The Parliament of Israel* (New York: Herzl Press 1967). Zidon's is the most comprehensive study available. It describes in detail the relationship between the Knesset and public administration, including a short chapter (23) on the State Comptroller. Another institutional study is that by Henry E. Baker, *The Legal System of Israel* (London: Sweet and Maxwell, 1961).

Studies of the administrative culture in the first decade of the state's existence were concerned with its overwhelming problems and the continuity of administrative arrangements: S. Mailick, "Organization for Personnel Management in Israel," *Public Personnel Review*, 28-35 (January 1952); also Edwin Samuel, "Israel's

Administrative Problems," *Zionist Quarterly*, 3 (Winter
1952); O.E. Ault, *Report on Training of the Civil Service of Israel* (New York: United Nations Technical Assistance Program, 1953); J.D. Corovan, *A Plan for Strengthening Public Administration in Israel* (Chicago: Public
Administration Service, 1953); D. Arian, "First Five
Years of the Israeli Civil Service," *Scripta Hierosolymi-
tana*, 3: 340-377 (1956); Edwin Samuel, "A New Civil Service for Israel," *Public Administration* (London) 34:
135-141 (Summer 1956); Edwin Samuel, *British Traditions
in the Administration of Israel* (Jerusalem: Rubin Mass,
1957); M.G. Goodrick, *Management in the Government of
Israel* (United States Operative Mission to Israel, 1958);
D. Roselio, *Ten Years of the Israeli Civil Service*
(Jerusalem: 1959); and Yehezkel Dror, "Some Aspects of
Staff Problems in Israel," in *Staff Problems in Tropical
and Subtropical Countries* (International Institute of
Differing Civilizations, 1961), pp. 293-321.

By the end of the first decade, primary sources had
become more plentiful and were joined by several journals
of continuing importance that were devoted to administra-
tion: *Knesset Record* (Divrei ha Knesset) 1949-; *Law Book*
(Sefer Ha-Huqim) 1949-; *Records of Proposed Bills*
(Reshumot; Haza'ot Hols) 1949-; *Official Gazette* (Iton
Rishmi) 1948-; *Government Yearbook* (Shenaton Ha
Memshalah) 1948-; *Treasury of Judgments* (Ozor Pisquei
Din) 1950-; and *Statistical Abstract of Israel*, 1947.
In addition, there are the annual reports of all national
institutions (including the Jewish Agency, Histadrut,
ministries, local governments, public corporations, pri-
vate companies, banks and political movements), particu-
larly the publications of the State Comptroller and Civil
Service Commission. The most relevant journals include
HaMinahel (Hebrew), *Netivey Irgun Ve'Minhal* (Hebrew),
Public Administration in Israel and Abroad, and *HaMiphal*
(Hebrew).

Among the important secondary sources of the past
decade, other than articles reproduced from these Israeli
journals, there is Benjamin Akzin and Yehezkel Dror,

118

Israel: High Pressure Planning (Syracuse University Press, 1966), a pioneering work with an introduction "Planning as Crisis Management" by B.M. Gross. It covers in detail much of the planning efforts in Israel and should now be supplemented by E. Spiegal, *New Towns in Israel* (Stuttgart: 1966); L. Laufer, *Israel and the Developing Countries: New Approaches to Cooperation* (New York: The Twentieth Century Fund, 1967); and some of the more insightful accounts of the Six Day War. Professor Dror has been active in promoting public policy analysis in Israel and has produced several papers on this topic, obtainable from the Department of Political Science, Kaplan School, Hebrew University, Jerusalem and the RAND Corporation, Santa Monica, California.

Other relevant works include E. Katz and S.N. Eisenstadt, "Observations on the Responses of Israeli Organizations to New Immigrants," *Administrative Science Quarterly*, 5: 1 (1960); Gerald E. Caiden, "Prospects for Administrative Reform in Israel," *Public Administration* (London) 25-46 (Spring 1968); Gerald E. Caiden and Nimrod Raphaeli, "Some Current Personnel Problems in the Israeli Civil Service," *Public Personnel Review*, 106-110 (April 1968); "The Ombudsman Debate in Israeli Politics," *Parliamentary Affairs* (Summer 1968); "The Politicization of Israeli Bureaucracy," *Canadian Journal of Public Administration*, forthcoming; and *Student Perception of Public Administration in Israel: A Survey* (Department of Political Science, Kaplan School, Hebrew University, Jerusalem), forthcoming.